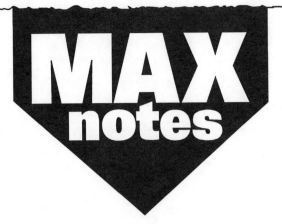

William Shakespeare's

Romeo and Juliet

Text by
Judy Clamon
(M.A., East Texas State University)
Department of English
Mabank High School
Mabank, Texas

D1316174

Research & Education Association

MAXnotes® for
ROMEO AND JULIET

Year 2005 Printing

Printed in the United States of America

Library of Congress Control Number 98-68781

International Standard Book Number 0-87891-990-2

MAXnotes® and REA® are registered trademarks of Research & Education Association, Inc., Piscataway, New Jersey 08854

C05

What **MAXnotes**® *Will Do for You*

This book is intended to help you absorb the essential contents and features of William Shakespeare's *Romeo and Juliet* and to help you gain a thorough understanding of the work. The book has been designed to do this more quickly and effectively than any other study guide.

For best results, this **MAXnotes** book should be used as a companion to the actual work, not instead of it. The interaction between the two will greatly benefit you.

To help you in your studies, this book presents the most up-to-date interpretations of every section of the actual work, followed by questions and fully explained answers that will enable you to analyze the material critically. The questions also will help you to test your understanding of the work and will prepare you for discussions and exams.

Meaningful illustrations are included to further enhance your understanding and enjoyment of the literary work. The illustrations are designed to place you into the mood and spirit of the work's settings.

The **MAXnotes** also include summaries, character lists, explanations of plot, and section-by-section analyses. A biography of the author and discussion of the work's historical context will help you put this literary piece into the proper perspective of what is taking place.

The use of this study guide will save you the hours of preparation time that would ordinarily be required to arrive at a complete grasp of this work of literature. You will be well prepared for classroom discussions, homework, and exams. The guidelines that are included for writing papers and reports on various topics will prepare you for any added work which may be assigned.

The **MAXnotes** will take your grades "to the max."

Larry B. Kling
Chief Editor

Contents

> **Each scene includes List of Characters,**
> **Summary, Analysis, Study Questions and**
> **Answers, and Suggested Essay Topics.**

MAXnotes® are simply the best – but don't just take our word for it...

"... I have told every bookstore in the area to carry your MAXnotes. They are the only notes I recommend to my students. There is no comparison between MAXnotes and all other notes ..."
    – High School Teacher & Reading Specialist,
    Arlington High School, Arlington, MA

"... I discovered the MAXnotes when a friend loaned me her copy of the *MAXnotes for Romeo and Juliet*. The book really helped me understand the story. Please send me a list of stores in my area that carry the MAXnotes. I would like to use more of them ..."
    – Student, San Marino, CA

"... The two MAXnotes titles that I have used have been very, very useful in helping me understand the subject matter reviewed. Thank you for creating the MAXnotes series ..."
    – Student, Morrisville, PA

A Glance at Some of the Characters

Romeo

Juliet

Mercutio

Nurse

Lord Capulet

Friar Laurence

Tybalt

Paris

SECTION ONE

Introduction

The Life and Work of William Shakespeare

Details about William Shakespeare's life are sketchy, mostly mere surmise based upon court or other clerical records. His parents, John and Mary (Arden), were married about 1557; she was of the landed gentry, and he a yeoman—a glover and commodities merchant. By 1568, John had risen through the ranks of town government and held the position of high bailiff, similar to mayor. William, the eldest son and the third of eight children, was born in 1564, probably on April 23, several days before his baptism on April 26 in Stratford-upon-Avon. Shakespeare is also believed to have died on the same date—April 23—in 1616.

It is believed William attended the local grammar school in Stratford where his parents lived, and studied primarily Latin rhetoric, logic, and literature. At age 18 (1582), William married Anne Hathaway, a local farmer's daughter who was eight years his senior. Their first daughter (Susanna) was born six months later (1583), and twins Judith and Hamnet were born in 1585.

Shakespeare's life can be divided into three periods: the first 20 years in Stratford, which include his schooling, early marriage, and fatherhood; the next 25 years as an actor and playwright in London; and the last five in retirement back in Stratford where he enjoyed moderate wealth gained from his theatrical successes. The years linking the first two periods are marked by a lack of information about Shakespeare, and are often referred to as the "dark years."

Shakespeare probably left school at age 15, which was the norm, to take a job, especially since this was the period of his father's financial difficulty. Numerous references in his plays suggest that William may have in fact worked for his father, in addition to a myriad of other jobs, thereby gaining specialized knowledge.

At some point during the "dark years," Shakespeare began his career with a London theatrical company, perhaps in 1589, for he was already an actor and playwright of some note by 1592.

Shakespeare apparently wrote and acted for numerous theatrical companies, including Pembroke's Men, and Strange's Men, which later became the Chamberlain's Men, with whom he remained for the rest of his career.

In 1592, the Plague closed the theaters for about two years, and Shakespeare turned to writing book length narrative poetry. Most notable were "Venus and Adonis" and "The Rape of Lucrece," both of which were dedicated to the Earl of Southampton, whom scholars accept as Shakespeare's friend and benefactor despite a lack of documentation. During this same period, Shakespeare was writing his sonnets, which are more likely signs of the time's fashion rather than actual love poems detailing any particular relationship. He returned to playwriting when theaters reopened in 1594, and did not continue to write poetry. His sonnets were published without his consent in 1609, shortly before his retirement.

Amid all of his success, Shakespeare suffered the loss of his only son, Hamnet, who died in 1596 at the age of 11.

But Shakespeare's career continued unabated; and in London in 1599, he became one of the partners in the new Globe Theater, which was built by the Chamberlain's Men.

When Queen Elizabeth died in 1603 and was succeeded by her cousin King James of Scotland, the Chamberlain's Men was renamed the King's Men. Shakespeare's productivity and popularity continued uninterrupted. He invested in London real estate and, one year away from retirement, purchased a second theater, the Blackfriars Gatehouse, in partnership with his fellow actors.

Shakespeare wrote very little after 1612, which was the year he completed *Henry VIII*. It was during a performance of this play in 1613 that the Globe caught fire and burned to the ground. Sometime between 1610 and 1613, Shakespeare returned to Stratford, where he owned a large house and property, to spend his remaining years with his family.

William Shakespeare died on April 23, 1616, and was buried two days later in the chancel of Holy Trinity Church where he had been baptized exactly 52 years earlier. His literary legacy included 37 plays, 154 sonnets and five major poems.

Incredibly, most of Shakespeare's plays had never been published in anything except pamphlet form, and were simply extant as acting scripts stored at the Globe. Theater scripts were not regarded as literary works of art, but only the basis for the performance. Plays were simply a popular form of entertainment for all layers of society in Shakespeare's time. Only the efforts of two of Shakespeare's company, John Heminges and Henry Condell, preserved his 36 plays (minus *Pericles,* the thirty-seventh).

Historical Background

The first permanent professional theater in England was built around 1576 and was called the Theater. Other theaters soon opened, including two called the Curtain and the Rose. Not only was Shakespeare working as a playwright and an actor for the Theater, he was also a stock holder.

Another theater soon opened and became one of the most famous of the London public playhouses. It was completed around 1599 and was called the Globe. It was perhaps the largest theater in England and derived its name "from the sign painted above its door, a picture of Atlas holding the world on his shoulders" (Kittredge). Shakespeare also owned stock in the Globe and performed as an actor in many of his own plays. The Globe was an enclosed theater without a roof. The spectators who stood or sat on the ground around the acting area were called "groundlings." The wealthier playgoers sat in galleries surrounding the stage area. There was no curtain, and sunlight provided the lighting for the performances; therefore, the performances were held during the day. Because there were no sets or scene changes, Shakespeare's characters wore extravagant costumes to provide the beauty and pageantry that was expected on the stage. Plays were usually fast-paced and colorful productions. The actors, as a rule, played more than one part in a play, and all of the women's parts were portrayed by young boys.

Shakespeare began writing comedies from about 1594 to 1603. During this period he produced such works as *The Taming of the Shrew, Two Gentlemen of Verona, A Midsummer-Night's Dream, The Merchant of Venice, Much Ado About Nothing,* and *Twelfth Night.* Two of Shakespeare's tragedies were also written during this time period. One was *Julius Caesar* and the other was *Romeo and Juliet.*

The play version of *Romeo and Juliet* was probably written early in his career around 1595 to 1596. The play is considered to be a tragedy and portrays the interplay of human character and motive. Much of *Romeo and Juliet* is written in blank verse, which is unrhymed iambic pentameter. Iambic simply means a metrical foot made up of an unstressed and stressed syllable, and pentameter means that each line has five metrical feet. While most of *Romeo and Juliet* is written in iambic pentameter, the characters of lower social position speak in prose.

The play is rich in rhyming words, word plays, and puns. Most of Shakespeare's plays begin with a great deal of action designed to capture the attention of the groundlings immediately. Therefore, *Romeo and Juliet* begins with a street fight between the servants of the Capulets and the Montagues, the warring families in the play.

The plot of *Romeo and Juliet* was taken from an earlier version of the story. The theme appeared in the fourth century in a Greek tale and later in the sixteenth century as Luigi da Porto's *Hystoria di due nobili Amanti.* In the later version, the city is Verona, and da Porto was the first to call the hero and heroine Romeo and Giulietta. Probably Shakespeare's most direct source was a long English narrative poem written in 1562 by Arthur Brooke, called *The Tragicall Historye of Romeus and Juliet.* Shakespeare used the characters in Brooke's poem but developed them in much greater depth and detail, thus transforming the story of star-crossed lovers into the most famous love story ever known.

Master List of Characters

Friends and Relatives of the Montague Family:

Romeo—*Son of Montague who falls in love with Juliet*

Montague—*Head of the family who is at war with the Capulets and father to Romeo*

Lady Montague—*Wife to Lord Montague and mother to Romeo*

Mercutio—*A kinsman to the prince and a friend to Romeo*

Benvolio—*A gentle and peace-loving young man who is nephew to Montague and a friend to Romeo*

Balthasar—*A loyal friend and servant to Romeo*

Abram—*A servant of the Montague family*

Friends and Relatives of the Capulet Family:

Juliet—*Daughter of Capulet who falls in love with Romeo*

Tybalt—*A fiery tempered young man who is the nephew of Lady Capulet and cousin to Juliet*

Capulet—*Head of the family who is at war with the Montagues and father to Juliet*

Lady Capulet—*Wife to Lord Capulet and mother to Juliet*

Nurse—*A witty nurse and friend to Juliet*

Sampson—*A servant of the Capulet family*

Gregory—*A servant of the Capulet family*

Peter—*A servant to Juliet's nurse*

Other Characters:

Chorus—*Introduces the play, and sets scene in Acts I and II*

Paris—*Kinsman to the prince and a young nobleman who asks for Juliet's hand in marriage*

Escalus—*The prince of Verona*

Friar Laurence—*A Franciscan friar who marries the lovers in hopes of making peace with the two warring families*

Friar John—*A Franciscan friar who was entrusted with an important letter to Romeo*

Apothecary—*A poor druggist in Mantua who sells poison to Romeo*

Page—*A servant to Paris*

Summary of the Play

The play opens with the servants of the Montague and Capulet families quarreling and fighting in the streets of Verona, Italy. The two families have been enemies for as long as anyone can remember. Romeo, son of Lord Montague, accidentally finds out about a ball given by Lord Capulet and plans to attend uninvited. Romeo and his friends Mercutio and Benvolio put on masks and attend the ball, where Romeo meets the beautiful Juliet and falls instantly in love. Later that night Romeo goes to Juliet's balcony and they exchange vows of love. Romeo enlists the help of Friar Laurence, who agrees to marry the young lovers in hopes of ending the longstanding feud between the two families.

Romeo returns from his wedding and finds that his friend Mercutio is engaged in combat with Tybalt, a member of the Capulet family. Tybalt kills Mercutio. Romeo, enraged over his friend's death, then slays Tybalt. Romeo immediately realizes that he has murdered his wife's cousin and flees to Friar Laurence for help. He also learns that the Prince has banned him from the city under penalty of death if he is found within its borders. Friar Laurence arranges for Romeo to spend one last night with Juliet before he flees to Mantua.

In the meantime, Lord Capulet, unaware that Juliet is married to Romeo, has promised her hand in marriage to Paris. When Juliet is told of the arranged marriage, she is desperate and seeks the help of Friar Laurence, who gives her a vial of sleeping potion. The potion will have a death-like but temporary effect. The plan is for Juliet to take the potion, appear to be dead, and be laid out in the family vault. Romeo will come to the vault the next night, and be there waiting when she awakens. The couple will then flee to Mantua to live. Friar Laurence sends the important message to Romeo telling him of his plan to help Juliet, but the message never reaches Romeo. Juliet, assured by Friar Laurence that Romeo will be waiting for her when she awakens in the tomb, goes home and drinks the potion.

Hearing that Juliet is dead, Romeo purchases poison from a poor apothecary and rushes to her tomb. Upon his arrival, he finds Paris, also in mourning. Thinking that Romeo has come to rob the tomb, Paris fights with Romeo. Romeo kills Paris, enters into the tomb, and buries Paris there. He then bids farewell to Juliet and takes the poison. Awakening from her death-like sleep, Juliet discovers her dead lover and kills herself with Romeo's dagger. Friar Laurence arrives too late to save the lovers and tells the Prince the entire story. The Montagues and Capulets promise to end their hostilities, which have caused the deaths of their only children.

Estimated Reading Time

Because of the play form and the language of Shakespeare, an average student should spend about an hour per act in individual reading. Each act may be broken down into two or three scenes at a time to ensure understanding. The language might be difficult at first, and will require careful examination of footnotes or helps located in the text. After reading each scene, you should answer all study questions in relation to that scene to ensure understanding and comprehension. The essay questions may be used if needed. Since there are five acts in *Romeo and Juliet*, you should expect to spend approximately five hours divided in segments of eight to ten sessions.

Act I

Act I, Scenes 1 and 2

New Characters:

Chorus

Sampson: *a servant in the Capulet household*

Gregory: *a servant in the Capulet household*

Benvolio: *a peace-loving friend to Romeo and the Montague family*

Tybalt: *a fiery-tempered member of the Capulet family*

Lord Capulet: *the head of the Capulet household*

Lady Capulet: *the wife of Lord Capulet and mother of Juliet*

Lord Montague: *the head of the Montague household*

Lady Montague: *the wife of Lord Montague and the mother of Romeo*

Prince Escalus: *the Prince of Verona whose job is to keep the peace*

Romeo: *the tragic hero of the play who falls in love with the enemy's daughter, Juliet*

Paris: *the young nobleman who is asking Lord Capulet for Juliet's hand in marriage*

Servant: *a servant to the Capulet family who has been asked to deliver invitations to the ball*

Abram: *servant to Montague*

Summary

Before the action of Act I begins, the Chorus sets the stage with the Prologue, which summarizes the basic plot of the play. It states that two families in Verona have been bitter enemies for centuries. The fighting has broken out again between the families. A child from each of the warring families meet and fall in love, and it is the death of the children that finally ends the feud between the parents.

Scene 1 opens in Verona, Italy, with two Capulet servants walking down the street hoping to meet and start a fight with servants from the Montague family. Sampson decides to start the fight by biting his thumb at the Montague servants. This is an insulting gesture and sure to help start a quarrel. Gregory tells Sampson that he will back him up. They meet the Montague servants and a fight ensues. As the fighting progresses, even the townspeople take sides and become involved, resulting in a street brawl.

Benvolio enters and attempts to break up the fighting, but Tybalt also comes on the scene and challenges him to a duel. Just as Lord Capulet and Lord Montague call for their swords in order to enter into the fight, the Prince and his attendants arrive and break up the quarrel. The Prince threatens to execute anyone who breaks the peace with another brawl in Verona. He requests that Lord Capulet meet him privately and tells Lord Montague that he will talk with him that afternoon.

Benvolio relates the circumstances of the fight to Lord Montague. Lady Montague asks where Romeo is, and Benvolio tells her that he saw him out walking at dawn. Lord Montague is worried about Romeo and states that something is bothering him; however, no one can find out what it is. It seems that he has been seen walking in the night and at dawn with tears in his eyes; but, when the sun comes up, he retreats into his room and pulls the curtains against all light. Romeo approaches, and Benvolio promises to find out what is bothering him.

Benvolio meets Romeo and asks him what "sadness lengthens his (Romeo's) hours." Romeo replies that not having the love that he wants has made him unhappy. It seems that the woman he loves (Rosaline) has sworn not to fall in love. Benvolio encourages Romeo to forget her by comparing her beauty with that of other

girls in Verona. Romeo replies that a comparison with other girls would only make her appear even more beautiful. Benvolio states that he will get him to forget her or die trying.

Scene 2 also takes place on a street in Verona. Lord Capulet is discussing the recent brawl with Paris, a young nobleman. Capulet states that as old as he and Lord Montague are, it will not be too difficult to keep the peace.

Paris has asked for Juliet's hand in marriage and is asking for a reply from Lord Capulet. Lord Capulet tells Paris that he feels that thirteen is too young, but allows Paris to try to sway her into accepting his offer. If Juliet consents, Lord Capulet will also.

Lord Capulet tells Paris that he is giving an "old accustomed feast" this night and invites him to attend. Lord Capulet then hands an invitation list to a servant to deliver throughout the city, not realizing that the servant cannot read.

The servant is disgruntled because he cannot read the list and states that people should stick with what they know best. At that moment, Romeo and Benvolio enter, and the servant asks Romeo if he can read the list to him. Romeo reads the invitation list, and the servant invites him to attend the feast if he is not from the house of Montague. Romeo asks where the feast is to be held, and the servant replies that it is to be held at his master's house, the house of the "great rich Capulet."

Benvolio hears the name of Rosaline (the woman with whom Romeo thinks he is in love) on the list and persuades Romeo to attend the feast in order to compare the beauty of Rosaline with all the other beauties in Verona. Romeo agrees to go, but only to stand and stare at Rosaline.

Analysis

Before the action in Act I begins, Shakespeare uses a chorus to sum up or preview the plot of the play for the audience. The Chorus presents the Prologue of the play as a sonnet, and it serves three distinct purposes. First, it serves to introduce an atmosphere of conflict between two families which paradoxically yokes together the themes of love and violence. Second, it directs the reader's attention to the important part fate plays in the lives of the lovers. Third, it points out that the fate of the lovers is not within their control. The paradoxical theme of love and death, as announced in the Prologue, indicates the fate of the lovers with such words as "star-crossed," "fatal loins," and "death-marked love." The Prologue also establishes that the lovers are victims of both their parents' hate and an aggressive, violent society that regenerates itself with the breeding of more hate. The Prologue sums up the setting, the plot, the play's ending, the role of fate in the play's development, and the length of time the play will take on the Elizabethan stage.

The plot of *Romeo and Juliet* only encompasses five days in the lives of the characters, and it is important to follow closely the day on which each event occurs. Scenes 1 and 2 take place on the first day, and it is a Sunday at nine in the morning.

In Scene 1, the action of the play begins on the streets of Verona with the servants of the feuding families instigating a fight. The feud between the families is an ancient, bitter hatred that has affected the entire city and become a public issue. Even the townspeople of Verona have become involved in the fight. Shakespeare intended to begin his play with a street fight in order to appeal to the common people and immediately gain the attention of the groundlings who might become restless quickly.

The quarrel between the servants is an opportunity for Shakespeare to introduce the feud humorously. The Capulet servants banter as they swagger down Verona's streets. The play on words (choler-collar) delighted the Elizabethan audience. Shakespeare relieves the tension brought about by the fiery-tempered Tybalt through his use of humor. When Lord Capulet requests his long sword, his wife retorts, "A crutch, a crutch! Why call you for a sword?" She insinuates that because of his age, a crutch might be more appropriate.

Foreshadowing should be noted in the Prince's speech to the warring families. He states that brawling has broken out three times. Each fight has disturbed the "quiet of our streets" and caused the citizens of Verona to begin fighting again. The Prince's warning words are, "If ever you disturb our streets again, your lives shall pay the forfeit of the peace." He decrees that the punishment for future fighting will be death. The Prince is the voice of authority in Verona. His rule is absolute, and the consequences of his warning will surface in future scenes as the plot progresses.

The theme of love coexisting with hate or death is echoed in Shakespeare's word play and is vividly seen in the form of oxymorons in the following passage: "O brawling love! O loving hate!...O heavy lightness! serious vanity! / Mis-shapen chaos of well-seeming forms! / Feather of lead, bright smoke, cold fire, sick health! / Still-waking sleep...." The concepts of love and death or hate do not naturally go together, but represent opposites. Romeo uses these images to describe love. His selection of words also echo the strife of civil violence.

Since tragedy emphasizes character over fate, the characters become responsible for their own destruction. However, it is fate that manipulates the characters' decisions and development. Fate leads them into the circumstances that will ultimately help destroy them. Therefore, fate plays a tremendous part in the plot of *Romeo and Juliet*. Chance, coincidence, circumstance, and change are all dramatic means by which fate is given its influence in the play. The connection of character with the deed and the catastrophe sets the course of the tragedy, and its outcome is inevitable. The role of chance should be noted in such events as Lord Capulet giving the invitation list to a servant who cannot read, the servant asking Romeo to read the list of names and then inviting him to the feast, and Rosaline's appears on the invitation list. Benvolio then convinces Romeo to attend the ball in order to compare her beauty with the other girls who will be attending.

Romeo's character develops as he moves from a shallow infatuation for Rosaline to a mature romantic love for Juliet later in the play. In Act I, Romeo is portrayed as moody and melancholy. His "love" for Rosaline is not returned by her, and it has become a tormenting sickness to him. Benvolio asks, "What sadness lengthens Romeo's hours?" Romeo responds by saying, "Not having that which having makes them short." His unhappiness illustrates the emptiness of his love. Romeo, in Scene 2, is suffering and listless in his love for Rosaline. Benvolio makes a universal observation when he states, "Alas that love, so gentle in his view, should be so tyrannous and rough in proof." Benvolio points out that love is gentle in appearance but mean and rough in reality.

Love is illustrated in two different ways during the play. Not only is there a comparison of youthful, shallow love to the more mature love shared by Romeo and Juliet, but there is the love that is so overpowering that it seems to transcend all bounds of convention and reason. This type of love, experienced by Romeo and Juliet, is the opposite of the restricted, courtly love that is prevalent in fourteenth century Verona. Courtly love was governed by the customs and traditions of the time. According to custom, the young man must ask the father for the hand of his daughter in marriage. There was no such thing as a "love" marriage because the marriages were arranged by the fathers. Girls were betrothed to whomever their fathers chose, usually in alliances for family betterment. Many times the girl was extremely young. Juliet was not quite fourteen, and her mother says that she herself married at that age. The arranged marriage was based on family status and kinship. By asking Lord Capulet for Juliet's hand in marriage, Paris abides by all the rules of etiquette and is in harmony with social expectations. On the other hand, Romeo will break all the conventional rules with his impulsiveness and his own values not subject to time or custom.

Study Questions

1. What is the setting for the play?

2. What scene of conflict opens the action of the play?

3. Which character tries to stop the fighting among the servants?

4. Which character is aggressive and eager to fight?

5. What warning does the Prince give to anyone who breaks the peace again?

6. Who has asked for Juliet's hand in marriage?

7. How old is Juliet?

8. In what state of mind is Romeo when we first see him in the play?

9. Explain how Romeo finds out about the Capulet ball.

10. How does Benvolio try to remedy Romeo's love sickness?

Answers

1. The setting is a street scene in Verona, Italy.

2. The play opens with a conflict between the Capulet and Montague servants. Eventually, even the townspeople become involved.

3. Benvolio tries to stop the fighting among the servants.

4. Tybalt is aggressive and eager to fight. He challenges Benvolio to draw his sword.

5. The Prince decrees that if anyone breaks the peace again, he shall pay with his life.

6. Paris has asked for Juliet's hand in marriage.

7. Juliet is thirteen years old.

8. As the play opens, Romeo's state of mind can best be described as love-sick, in love with love, moody, and melancholy.

9. Romeo finds out about the Capulet ball when an illiterate Capulet servant asks him to read the invitation list to him.

10. Benvolio tries to remedy Romeo's love-sickness by getting him to consent to go to the Capulet ball and examine other beauties.

Suggested Essay Topics

1. Explain the operation of fate and how it has worked in Scenes 1 and 2 of the play to help bring the two lovers together.

2. Explain the rules of marriage during the fourteenth century.

3. What major conflicts are established in the first scene?

4. Explain the purpose of the Prologue.

Act I, Scenes 3-5

New Characters:

Nurse: *Juliet's nurse who has taken care of her since her infancy*

Susan: *the Nurse's daughter who was born on the same day as Juliet but died. She is not in the scene but is alluded to by the Nurse*

Mercutio: *a friend to Romeo who loves words*

Summary

In Scene 3 Lady Capulet informs Juliet that it is time for her to think of marriage. At first Lady Capulet sends the Nurse away, but then calls her back, remembering that she knows all their secrets anyway. The Nurse and Lady Capulet discuss Juliet's age; and the Nurse recalls exactly the hour of Juliet's birth because she was born on Lammas Eve, the same day as Susan, her daughter who died.

Lady Capulet asks Juliet if she is ready to marry. Juliet replies that she has not even thought of marriage. Lady Capulet tells her about Paris and compares him to a book that only needs a cover (a wife). Lady Capulet stresses his physical attractiveness and his wealth, which enforce the belief that love dwells in the eye rather than in the heart. Juliet, always obedient to her parents, agrees to look at him at the feast that night and to consider his suit.

Scene 4 portrays Romeo and his friends on their way to the ball. The young men are carrying or wearing masks. Benvolio suggests that they enter quietly, dance, and then leave. Mercutio is a glib speaker and loves to hear himself talk. He is light-hearted and ridicules Romeo's love-sickness. He (Mercutio) delivers a speech about Queen Mab, the queen of fairyland, and what she is able to do to dreamers. Romeo has a premonition that something is about to happen that will shorten his life, but decides that he must go forward regardless.

The setting in Scene 5 is within the Capulet house. The servants are busy preparing for the ball. Lord Capulet, jolly and remembering his youth, welcomes everyone and intimidates the young women into dancing with him by saying that "Ladies that have their toes unplagued with corns will walk about (dance) with

you." If any young lady refuses to dance with him, he swears to tell everyone that she has corns on her feet.

Romeo sees Juliet for the first time and falls instantly in love. His tortured love for Rosaline has been replaced with a blissful love for Juliet. He compares her beauty to the brightness of torches, a rich jewel in an Ethiop's ear, and a snowy dove. As he speaks of her beauty, Tybalt recognizes his voice and knows that he is a Montague. Tybalt sends for his sword only to be stopped by Lord Capulet, who warns him not to disrupt his ball with a fight. Lord Capulet allows Romeo to remain at the feast because he is behaving like a gentleman, Verona speaks well of him, and he does not want the joy of his ball disrupted. Tybalt is furious that Romeo is allowed to stay and storms out. Romeo and Juliet speak to one another using words such as "pilgrim," "saint," "palmers," "devotions," and "shrines"—all holy terms. Juliet is called away to her mother, and Romeo asks the Nurse who she is. He is told that she is a Capulet, and he realizes that his "life is my foe's debt." As Romeo and his friends leave the feast, Juliet asks the Nurse who he is. The Nurse tells her that "His name is Romeo, and a Montague, / The only son of your great enemy." It is this knowledge that makes Juliet say, "My only love sprung from my only hate! / Too early seen unknown, and known too late!"

Analysis

When Juliet's mother comes to discuss marriage with her and sends the Nurse away, the nurse feels disappointment and hurt. The Nurse has been more of a mother to Juliet than Lady Capulet. The Nurse and Lady Capulet are opposites in nature. The nurse exhibits complete ease with Juliet. She is earthy, a little bawdy, and very frank with her opinions, advice, and feelings. On the other hand, Lady Capulet is stiff and reserved with her daughter. Juliet responds to the Nurse with gaiety and fondness, while her relationship with her mother is reserved, respectful, and timid. Juliet is the child the Nurse took in when her own baby died; thus, a very close relationship has developed between the two. The ties between Juliet and the nurse go far beyond master and servant. Never discouraged by the Capulet family, the Nurse has taken on the role of companion, confidant, friend, mother, and co-conspirator.

It should be noted that Juliet is polite and obedient to her parents. Chastity, silence, and obedience were three virtues expected of both daughters and wives in the Elizabethan period. Juliet's defiance later in the play becomes a sign of the unconventionality of her love and its transforming powers. In Act I, Juliet respects the wishes of her parents and strives to please them, even if it means marrying someone they have chosen for her. When her mother discusses marriage with her, she is respectful, obedient, but indifferent. Her attitude will change as the play progresses and she becomes more of a woman.

Elizabethan spectators enjoyed humor, and Shakespeare does not disappoint them. Humor relieves tension built by intense moments in the script, and it also provides entertainment for the audience, especially the groundlings who might become restless if the action did not move rapidly. Shakespeare employs humor when old Lord Capulet, who is reliving his youth, threatens to tell everyone that any young lady who refuses to dance with him has corns on her feet. It is also used when Benvolio teases Romeo about his love-sickness. The Nurse's constant chatter when Lady Capulet tries to talk to Juliet about marriage, a serious subject, also provides additional humor in these scenes.

While humor and lightheartedness are important, images are equally important in building the total impression of the play, and these should be noted in the first act. As Lady Capulet appeals to Juliet to consider marriage to Paris, she uses the comparison of Paris to a fine book. Lady Capulet says, "Read o'er the volume of young Paris' face, and find delight writ there with beauty's pen.... And what obscur'd in this fair volume lies/ Find written in the margin of his eyes./ This precious book of love, this unbound lover,/ To beautify him only lacks a cover." The comparison is very formal and conventional.

The love that Romeo and Juliet share is sprinkled with religious imagery as well as light imagery. The words that Romeo and Juliet speak to one another upon first meeting are filled with religious meanings and undertones. The first 14 lines of their conversation is a sonnet consisting of references to worship. Juliet is the saint, and Romeo is the pilgrim. The imagery is illustrated with the following discussion between Romeo and Juliet. Romeo says, "If I

profane with my unworthiest hand/ This holy shrine, the gentle fine is this:/My lips, two blushing pilgrims, ready stand/ To smooth that rough touch with a tender kiss." Juliet replies, "Good pilgrim, you do wrong your hand too much,/ Which mannerly devotion shows in this;/ For saints have hands that pilgrims' hands do touch,/ And palm to palm is holy palmers' kiss." The devotion that Romeo and Juliet show for one another is pure and holy, unlike the infatuation that he had felt so recently for Rosaline.

Throughout the play there is a contrast between light and dark images. Rosaline becomes associated with darkness and Juliet with lightness. The imagery of light is illustrated by such comparisons as Juliet's beauty to the brightness of torches, jewels, and a "snowy dove trooping with crows."

Mercutio is a key character in the play. He believes in taking action and in being realistic. He entertains his friends with his nimble wit and use of puns, figurative language, and word play. Mercutio's speech is both imaginative and filled with imagery as he describes the work of Queen Mab on sleeping people. He becomes carried away with his witty fantasy on dreams and has to be stopped by Romeo. Mercutio is used as a foil or contrast to Romeo. This contrast makes the particular qualities of each character stand out vividly. At this point in the play, Romeo is focused on his inner life and his emotions, while Mercutio is focused on entertaining others with his wit. Romeo is melancholy and fatalistic while Mercutio is cheerful and confident.

Through instances of chance, coincidence, circumstance, and change, the theme of fate in the lives of Romeo and Juliet is continued in Scenes 3, 4, and 5. Romeo was persuaded by Benvolio to attend the ball. He consents to go only to watch Rosaline, not knowing that he will meet his only true love—Juliet. Juliet, on the other hand, is present at the ball supposedly observing Paris, a prospective husband. Both Romeo and Juliet fall instantly in love with one another. It is also fate that Lord Capulet refuses to allow Tybalt to vent his anger against Romeo, and even allows Romeo to remain at the ball.

Foreshadowing anticipates what will come to pass, and thus reinforces the sense of fate at work in the play. There are three examples of foreshadowing in this act. The Prince's speech in Scene

1 warns that death will be the penalty if the city's peace is again disturbed by the feuding families. In Scene 4, Romeo has a premonition of something evil happening, "some consequence, yet hanging in the stars," but he feels that he can do nothing to prevent it from occurring. He believes that fate has complete control of his destiny and this premonition echoes the "star-crossed lovers" mentioned in the Prologue. The third example of foreshadowing is in Scene 5 when Tybalt delivers his warning as he leaves his uncle's feast. He states, "I will withdraw; but this intrusion shall,/ No seeming sweet, convert to bitt'rest gall." Tybalt vows to seek revenge upon Romeo for daring to attend the Capulet ball.

As a whole, Act I provides the reader with the introduction or exposition. It creates the tone of the play which allows the audience to know the dangers associated with a romance between a Capulet and a Montague. It presents the co-existing concepts of love and hate that are present not only within these two warring families, but in society at the time. Act I also defines the setting and introduces most of the characters.

Study Questions

1. Who is Susan?

2. When is Juliet's birthday?

3. Why does Lady Capulet visit with Juliet? What questions does she ask her?

4. How do the Nurse and Lady Capulet feel about Paris?

5. Which character loves to talk?

6. Who is Queen Mab?

7. What premonition does Romeo have?

8. How did Lord Capulet force the young ladies to dance with him?

9. Who recognizes Romeo's voice at the feast and becomes furious because he is allowed to stay?

10. Who first tells Romeo and Juliet who the other is?

Answers

1. Susan is the Nurse's daughter who was born on the same day as Juliet; however, she died.

2. Juliet's birthday is on Lammas Eve.

3. Lady Capulet visits with Juliet to ask her if she is ready for marriage. She asks Juliet to look at Paris at the feast that night.

4. The Nurse and Lady Capulet feel that Paris is a perfect match for Juliet and are in favor of the marriage.

5. Mercutio loves to talk and uses figurative language and many plays on words.

6. Queen Mab is the Queen of Fairies. She is responsible for what men dream.

7. Romeo has a premonition that something is about to happen that will shorten his life.

8. Lord Capulet threatens to tell everyone that any young lady who does not dance with him has corns on her feet.

9. Tybalt recognizes Romeo's voice and becomes furious when Lord Capulet allows him to remain at the ball.

10. The Nurse is the one who identifies each of the lovers.

Suggested Essay Topics

1. Compare the love that Romeo feels for Juliet to the love that he felt for Rosaline.

2. Explain the imagery of light and dark in Act I and how it is used as symbols for Rosaline and Juliet.

3. How does Shakespeare use humor in Act I?

4. Trace how fate has brought the two lovers together.

Act II

Act II, Scenes 1 and 2

Summary

    Act II begins with another Prologue in the form of a sonnet which provides the audience with a preview of what is to come. It states that the shallow love that Romeo had for Rosaline has been replaced with love for Juliet. "Alike bewitched by the charm of looks" expresses that both Romeo and Juliet are mutually attracted to one another. His feelings are returned and "passion lends them power."

    Scene 1 takes place outside the walls of Lord Capulet's house. Romeo feels that he can not leave because his heart remains where Juliet lives, and he climbs over the wall into the orchard. Romeo's friends, who do not know of Romeo's new love, call for him and try to entreat him to come out of hiding by calling out Rosaline's name. Mercutio teases Romeo about Rosaline, not realizing that her name now means nothing to him. Romeo's friends give up looking for him and return to their homes.

    Scene 2 takes place within the walls of Lord Capulet's orchard. Romeo watches as Juliet appears at her window and compares her to light, the East, the sun, and the stars in heaven. As she leans her cheek upon her hand, he wishes that he could be a glove on the hand that touches her cheek. He listens as she calls out his name, and he hears her proclaim that it is only his name that is her enemy. Romeo jumps from the bushes and declares that he will change his name if that is keeping her from loving him. Juliet is startled and surprised that he has heard her secret thoughts. She asks how he was able to get over the high orchard walls and find

her. To this, Romeo answers that love helped him accomplish both. Juliet is concerned that she has been too forward with him. She promises that she will be more true than any girl who acts shy and distant. Romeo tries to swear on the moon that he loves her; however, Juliet begs him not to swear on something that changes so frequently. The two lovers exchange vows of love, and Juliet asks if his intentions are honorable. If they are, when should she send someone to get the information concerning the time and place for their wedding. Romeo tells her to send someone at nine o'clock in the morning for the details. The Nurse calls to Juliet, interrupting their balcony love scene. As Romeo prepares to leave, Juliet says her famous lines, "Good night, good night! Parting is such sweet sorrow /That I shall say good night till it be morrow."

Analysis

These two scenes, which show that Benvolio and Mercutio believe Romeo is still playing a love game, and which isolate the lovers from family and friends, are probably the most well known scenes in the play. Some of the most poetic language is found here in the form of images, figures of speech, and the music of the lines.

Romeo's soliloquy, a dramatic monologue spoken aloud to reveal a the character's thoughts, is found in the first part of Scene 2. The monologue conveys an idealized quality of their love and clearly describes his new feeling for Juliet in terms of brightness. He even states that the brightness of her eyes, if up in heaven, would light up the skies and make the birds think it was day. He again uses imagery of light and dark when he first sees Juliet on the balcony and states, "What light through yonder window breaks?/ It is the East, and Juliet is the sun!/Arise, fair sun, and kill the envious moon,/ Who is already sick and pale with grief." As Rosaline was compared to moon and night, Juliet is compared to sun, brightness, warmth, and light.

The famous lines, "O Romeo, Romeo! Wherefore art thou Romeo?" do not mean she is looking for him, but that she is asking why he is called Romeo and a Montague. She continues her speech declaring that if he cannot give up his name, she will give up her Capulet name. She then goes on to state that it is only his name that is her enemy, but not the person. She compares their love to lightning that ceases almost as soon as it is seen and to a bud that would bloom in time. This contrasting comparison illustrates the new meanings of love in each of their lives. Romeo is willing to face death in exchange for Juliet's love. The two lovers will repeatedly demonstrate that they prefer death to separation. Their entire relationship has been formed quickly. They have declared their love, exchanged vows, and plan to be married, all in a matter of hours. Possibly because both lovers realize the dangers of their love, they act quickly and impulsively.

Impulsive behavior is considered to be Romeo's tragic flaw (a weakness in a character that will cause his destruction). This flaw is first seen when Romeo quickly forgets Rosaline and turns his attentions to Juliet. He not only falls deeply in love with Juliet, but plans marriage, all within a matter of hours. While a certain amount of impetuosity is natural in the young, extremes can prove destructive for the characters.

Study Questions

1. Instead of returning home, where does Romeo go after the ball?

2. What is a soliloquy and how is it used in Scene 2?

3. By whose name does Mercutio call for Romeo?

4. How does Romeo learn of Juliet's love for him?

5. What does Romeo say helped him climb over the high walls of the Capulet orchard and find Juliet's window?

6. What do Romeo and Juliet exchange?

7. What do Romeo and Juliet plan to do the next day?

8. To what does Romeo compare Juliet's beauty?

9. Who keeps interrupting the balcony scene?

10. Why does Juliet ask Romeo not to swear by the moon?

Answers

1. After the ball, Romeo goes over the wall and into the Capulet orchard.

2. A soliloquy is a dramatic monologue spoken aloud by a character to reveal his thoughts to the audience. Romeo uses a soliloquy to describe Juliet's beauty as she stands on her balcony.

3. Mercutio keeps calling for Romeo in Rosaline's name.

4. He overhears Juliet speaking of her love for him when she thinks she is alone.

5. Love, which gave him wings, helped him over the wall and made it possible for him to find her balcony.

6. Romeo and Juliet exchange vows of love.

7. Romeo and Juliet plan to be married the next day.

8. Romeo compares Juliet's beauty to brightness, warmth, and light.

9. The Nurse keeps interrupting the balcony scene.

10. Juliet asks Romeo not to swear his love on the moon because the moon appears to change in size as it orbits the earth, suggesting that it is fickle.

Suggested Essay Topics

1. Explain how imagery and figures of speech make Scene 2 one of the most beautiful scenes in the play. Describe the imagery and figures of speech and illustrate how they are used.

2. Explain the purpose of Scenes 1 and 2.

3. Discuss Juliet's concerns in the balcony scene.

Act II, Scenes 3 and 4

New Characters:

Friar Laurence: *a Franciscan friar who is a priest and a specialist in herbs and medicines. He hopes that the marriage will end the feud between the two families.*

Peter: *the Nurse's servant*

Summary

As Scene 3 begins, the reader finds Friar Laurence carrying a wicker basket and selecting herbs, flowers, and plants to use in making medicine. It is daybreak on Monday, the second day in the lives of the lovers. Friar Laurence tells how plants contain both poisonous and healing powers. If a plant's use is abused, the result is harmful. "Virtue itself turns vice, being misapplied, / And vice sometime by action dignified." He applies this same lesson to man, who possesses both good and evil within him. If man allows the evil to become predominant in his life, it will destroy him.

Romeo approaches, and Friar Laurence asks if he is ill or if he has been up all night. Romeo answers that he has been up all night. To this, the Friar assumes that he has been with Rosaline and committed sin. Romeo assures him that this is not so and states that he has forgotten Rosaline. He reveals to the Friar that he has been with the daughter of Lord Capulet, and they have fallen in love and wish to be married today. The Friar scolds him for professing to love one woman one day and another on the next day. He states, "Young men's love then lies / Not truly in their hearts, but in their eyes." Romeo assures him that they both love one another. The Friar, hoping to end the feud by marrying the two lovers, agrees to marry them. As Romeo prepares to leave, the Friar worries about the haste of the marriage and says, "Wisely and slow. They stumble that run fast."

Scene 4 reveals Mercutio and Benvolio in the streets of Verona. They are discussing their love-sick friend who did not even go home last night after the ball. Benvolio says that Tybalt has sent a challenge to Romeo for a duel. Both friends wonder if Romeo will be able to handle a duel because he has been acting so strangely concerning Rosaline. His love-sickness has made him "already dead: stabbed with a white wench's black eye; run through the ear with a love song."

They are discussing Tybalt's expert fencing capabilities when Romeo appears. They tease Romeo about giving them the slip after the ball and about his love for Rosaline. As they banter words back and forth, the Nurse and her servant come on stage.

Mercutio makes fun of the Nurse with insulting words and she becomes angry. She asks for Romeo, and he identifies himself to

her. She says that Juliet has sent her for the marriage information. Romeo tells the Nurse that Juliet is to devise a reason to go to chapel that evening, and Friar Laurence will marry them. Romeo then tells her that his servant will give her a rope ladder to take back with her. Romeo will use the ladder to climb into Juliet's window later that night.

Analysis

Shakespeare's introduction of Friar Laurence gathering herbs is especially important to the plot of the play. Elizabethans were fascinated with potions and poisons, and the Friar's philosophical discourse on the power of medicinal plants and the similarities between plants and men enthralled them. The speech at the beginning of Scene 3 is a soliloquy stressing the dichotomy of nature and man and could be viewed as foreshadowing. Man, like many plants, does possess the capability of evil as well as good. Even the goodness in Romeo cannot overshadow his feelings of revenge later in the play. The Friar himself attempts to accomplish good by agreeing to unite the lovers in marriage, hoping that the alliance will end the feud between the families. Yet, the Friar acts rashly or impulsively when he agrees to the marriage. His intentions are good and honorable; however, he acts without considering the possible consequences of a secret marriage between members of feuding families. He cautions Romeo by saying that "Wisely and slow; they stumble that run fast." Then, he violates his own admonition by hastily agreeing to the marriage. Friar Laurence's hastiness is also a flaw within him that will aid in the destruction of the lovers.

Romeo's tragic flaw, impulsiveness, is recognized by the Friar who cautions him about acting too hastily. He reminds Romeo of his infatuation with Rosaline, which is so quickly forgotten. The Friar is an understanding and broadminded man who only tries to help by agreeing to the marriage.

Mercutio is again illustrated as a man of many words as he teases Romeo about Rosaline and love. As Mercutio and Benvolio discuss Romeo and the challenge sent by Tybalt, Mercutio is concerned about Romeo's ability to fight. "Alas, poor Romeo, he is already dead! / Stabb'd with a white wench's black eye; shot through / The ear with a love song; the very pin of his heart / Cleft with the

blind bow-boy's butt-shaft; and is he / A man to encounter Tybalt?" Mercutio has no idea that Romeo is no longer bothered with his former infatuation with Rosaline or that he has moved on to a new and deeper relationship with Juliet.

When the Nurse and Peter arrive upon the streets of Verona, Mercutio enjoys ridiculing her as well. She, in turn, reveals coarseness or vulgarity by saying, "I'll take him down,/ And 'a were lustier than he is, and twenty / Such Jacks; and if I cannot, I'll find those that shall./ Scurvy knave!" When she talks to Romeo, she tries to appear more ladylike by saying "I desire some confidence with you." She should have said, "conference." The use of a word that sounds like the one intended but is ridiculously wrong is called a malapropism and is used by Shakespeare in many of the Nurse's speeches.

The Nurse's love for Juliet prompts her to warn Romeo against hurting her. The Nurse plays an important part in advancing the plot of the play. She is closest to Juliet and enjoys being a part of the romantic plans of marriage. She is the important messenger of the details of the union, of when and where it will take place.

By the second day, the lovers have met, fallen in love, and plan to marry. The lovers are able to accomplish this with the help of the Nurse and the Friar, who have become accomplices.

Study Questions

1. What is Friar Laurence's special skill or area of knowledge?

2. With what does Friar Laurence compare the beneficial and poisonous parts of the plant?

3. About what does the Friar caution Romeo?

4. Why does the Friar agree to marry Romeo and Juliet?

5. Who has sent Romeo a challenge for a duel?

6. What excuse is Juliet to give for going to Friar Laurence's cell?

7. Where are Romeo and Juliet to be married?

8. Who teases Romeo about Rosaline and his love-sickness?

9. Who teases the Nurse and causes her to become crass?

10. How does Romeo plan to get into Juliet's window?

Answers

1. Friar Laurence's special skill is in making medicines and potions from herbs.

2. Friar Laurence compares the beneficial and poisonous parts of a plant to the good and evil within a man.

3. Friar Laurence cautions Romeo about being too hasty.

4. The Friar believes that by marrying the two lovers, he will end the feud between the Capulets and the Montagues.

5. Tybalt has sent Romeo a challenge for a duel. He is angry that Romeo came to the ball uninvited and was allowed to remain.

6. Juliet is going to get permission to go to Friar Laurence's cell by saying that she needs to go to shrift, or confession.

7. Romeo and Juliet are to be married in Friar Laurence's cell.

8. Mercutio, Romeo's friend, teases him about Rosaline and his love-sickness.

9. Mercutio teases the Nurse and causes her to become angry.

10. Romeo has given the Nurse a rope ladder in order that he might climb into Juliet's window later that night.

Suggested Essay Topics

1. Name the two other people in the play who know about the love between Romeo and Juliet and explain how they help the lovers achieve their goals.

2. Explain Friar Laurence's philosophy concerning the parts of a plant as compared to the potential actions of man.

3. Describe Mercutio and his role in the play.

Act II, Scenes 5 and 6

Summary

Scene 5 takes place within the Capulet orchard where Juliet is anxiously waiting for the Nurse to return with news from Romeo. The Nurse left at nine o'clock and it is now twelve. Juliet wishes that the Nurse were as in love as she is so that she would be faster in her return, for the waiting is torture for Juliet. The Nurse finally arrives, and Juliet says, "O Lord, why lookest thou sad? / Though news be sad, yet tell them merrily; / If good, thou shamest the music of sweet news / By playing it to me with so sour a face." The Nurse replies that her bones ache and asks that Juliet leave her alone for awhile. Juliet says, "I would thou hadst my bones, and I thy news." The Nurse banters with Juliet, claiming to be hot and too tired to talk. Then she tells Juliet that she has made a good choice. The Nurse finally asks Juliet if she is able to go to shrift today. If so, Romeo is waiting there to make her his wife.

Scene 6 takes place in Friar Laurence's cell where both he and Romeo are waiting for the arrival of Juliet. The Friar hopes that the future will not punish them with sorrow, and Romeo replies that sorrow cannot equal the joy that one minute in the sight of Juliet gives him. The Friar again cautions Romeo with the words, "Love moderately; long love doth so; Too swift arrives as tardy as too slow."

Juliet arrives and they both proclaim their immense love for one another. Juliet says, "But my true love is grown to such excess / I cannot sum up sum of half my wealth." At this point, the Friar performs the wedding ceremony.

Analysis

The love scenes are brought to a resolution as the friar marries the two lovers at the end of Scene 6. The relationship is further strengthened between Juliet and the Nurse as the nurse teases her about the wedding plans sent by Romeo. The Nurse is more the mother than Juliet's real mother—Lady Capulet. The nurse is immersed in Juliet's affairs and strives to help her with her plans. She approves of Romeo—his good looks and his polite mannerisms.

It is almost humorous the way Shakespeare allows the Nurse

to torment Juliet with her important news. "Now, good sweet nurse—O Lord, why look'st thou sad?/ Though news be sad, yet tell them merrily;/ If good, thou shamest the music of sweet news/ By playing it to me with so sour a face." The nurse replies, "I am aweary, give me leave awhile./ Fie, how my bones ache! What a jounce have I had!" Juliet says, " I would thou hadst my bones, and I thy news." As she complains about her weary bones, her tiredness, and her headache, Juliet is impatient to learn if and when she will be a bride.

The actual marriage ceremony is not included in the text. The beauty of the moment is presented as Romeo and Juliet exchange their love for one another, and the Friar states, "You shall not stay alone/ Till Holy Church incorporate two in one."

There was no such thing as a "love" marriage in the Elizabethan social culture. The marriages were arranged by the father, and the daughter was expected to be obedient to her parents in their requests. It should be noted that Paris was courting by the accepted rules of the day. He talked with the father first and asked for Juliet's hand in marriage. Paris is patient and waits for an answer from Lord Capulet. Romeo, on the other hand, does not court by the accepted rules. He has gone behind the father's back, talked directly with the daughter, and asks her to marry him. Not only has he not courted by the rules, the lovers are married secretly without the knowledge or consent of the parents.

It should also be noted that Juliet, like Romeo, is impatient and hasty in her decisions. She has abandoned all sense of reason and propriety and is ruled entirely by her impulses. She has fallen in love within the space of only a few hours and plans to marry within one day of meeting Romeo. Her impatience is also shown as she waits for the Nurse to return from seeing Romeo and again as she inquires about the meeting between the two.

Time, newly calculated or experienced in love's world is referred to in Juliet's soliloquy as she waits for the Nurse to return with the wedding news. Love has made time of great importance. Juliet's impatience and hastiness is illustrated as she waits for the Nurse to return from meeting with Romeo. She states, "Therefore do nimble-pinio'd doves draw Love,/ And therefore hath the wind-swift Cupid wings./ Now is the sun upon the highmost hill/ Of this

day's journey, and from nine till twelve/ Is three long hours; yet she is not come." Time has new meaning for Juliet. The love that she feels is unconventional and not a part of the regimented society of Verona.

Romeo has plunged into his new love impulsively. His passions completely absorb him and he has no thoughts of the consequences of his love for Juliet. His actions are not guided by reason, but by feelings alone. His willingness to face death is again acknowledged when Romeo states, "Then love-devouring death do what he dare—/ It is enough I may but call her mine." He does not realize that his lines touch upon the theme of love co-existing with death, or that they foreshadow the future for him and his new love.

Act II is where the complication or rising action takes place. Tension is created because of the conflict created when the children of two opposing families meet and fall in love. Additional conflicts are presented in the form of Tybalt challenging Romeo to a duel, and the actual marriage of Romeo and Juliet performed by Friar Laurence. This marriage intensifies the conflict, which in turn adds to the complication of Act II.

Study Questions

1. At what time did Juliet send the Nurse to see Romeo and find out the wedding plans?

2. How long has Juliet been waiting for the Nurse to return with the news from Romeo?

3. How does the Nurse react when she finally returns?

4. How does the Nurse feel about the marriage?

5. What is the Friar afraid of?

6. The friar warns Romeo again about something. What is it?

7. How much do the lovers say their love has grown?

8. How many people know of the marriage?

9. Where does the marriage take place?

10. What is another name for the Friar?

Answers

1. Juliet sent the Nurse at nine o'clock in the morning to find out the wedding news from Romeo.

2. Juliet has been waiting three hours for the Nurse to return with the news.

3. The Nurse teases Juliet by claiming to be tired from her journey and prolongs telling her the news.

4. The Nurse is in favor of the marriage and feels that Romeo is handsome as well as polite.

5. The Friar is afraid that both lovers are acting too hastily.

6. The Friar warns Romeo again about acting too hastily.

7. The lovers say that their love has grown to such an extent that it cannot be counted.

8. Four main characters know of the marriage. Romeo and Juliet, of course, are aware; but also the Nurse and Friar Laurence have become accomplices in the affair.

9. The marriage takes place in Friar Laurence's cell or chapel.

10. Friar Laurence is also referred to as the ghostly confessor.

Suggested Essay Topics

1. Explain the relationship between the Nurse and Juliet.

2. Explain the rules of courtship during this time period. Compare and contrast the actions of Paris and of Romeo in regard to courting and marriage.

3. Friar Laurence plays an important role in the lives of Romeo and Juliet. Explain his role in their lives—his concerns and his hopes.

Act III

Act III, Scenes 1 and 2

Summary

Scene 1 takes place on the streets of Verona. It is Monday afternoon on day two, about an hour after the wedding between Romeo and Juliet. Benvolio and Mercutio are walking down one of the streets when Benvolio suggests that they retire. The day is extremely hot, and if they meet with the Capulets, tempers will flare and there is bound to be a fight. Mercutio is ready for a fight and hopes to have one. The Capulets enter led by Tybalt, who inquires about Romeo. Tybalt had challenged Romeo to a duel to get revenge for his uninvited appearance at the Capulet ball. At this time, Romeo, who is returning from Friar Laurence's chapel, approaches the group of men.

Tybalt insults Romeo by calling him a villain, but Romeo responds by saying that Tybalt does not know him. To this, Tybalt challenges him to draw his sword, but Romeo replies, "I do protest I never injured thee, But love thee better than thou canst devise." Mercutio steps in to defend Romeo's honor and returns Tybalt's insult by calling him "Good King of Cats." Mercutio draws and he and Tybalt begin to fight. Romeo calls for Benvolio to help him stop the fight. Romeo reaches to push Mercutio away, thereby blocking Mercutio's view. Tybalt takes the opportunity to reach under Romeo's arm and fatally stabs Mercutio. When Romeo is told that Mercutio is dead, he realizes that his love for Juliet has made him act "effeminately." When Mercutio is killed, Romeo's sense of honor and loyalty leave him no choice but to avenge his friend's death.

He calls to Tybalt who returns and they fight. Romeo kills Tybalt and immediately realizes that he has murdered his new bride's cousin. Benvolio pleads with him to run and hide before he is found. The Prince comes to the public square and asks Benvolio the cause of the deaths. Benvolio relates the story, and the Prince exiles Romeo under penalty of death.

Scene 2 takes place late Monday afternoon. Juliet is anxiously waiting for night to come and with it, Romeo. The Nurse enters carrying the rope ladder and crying, "He's dead, he's dead, he's dead...O Romeo, Romeo! / Who ever would have thought it? Romeo!" Juliet mistakenly thinks that Romeo is dead. Then the Nurse begins calling out Tybalt's name and Juliet believes that both Romeo and Tybalt are dead. The Nurse finally tells her that Romeo killed Tybalt and has been banished by the Prince. Juliet, at first, feels betrayed by Romeo. Then her love for Romeo takes away the blame she felt against him. Juliet tells the Nurse that she will be weeping long after others have stopped weeping for Tybalt. She orders the Nurse to take a ring to Romeo as a token and to bid him come to her that night for a last farewell.

Analysis

Act I of the play is considered the introduction with Act II being the complication or rising action. Act III of the play is the climax or turning point. The turning point of a play takes place when something happens that turns the action of the play either toward a happy ending or toward a tragic ending. Romeo's killing of Tybalt is the turning point. Because of this act, Romeo will be banished, and there is no chance that he and Juliet will be able to reveal their marriage to their feuding parents. After the murders take place, the fate of the lovers is really out of their hands. Circumstances just carry the lovers into destruction and hopelessness.

Many of the characters have unknowingly aided in the rapidly approaching destruction of the lovers. Friar Laurence has contributed by hastily consenting to marry them without thinking about the consequences. The Nurse, through love for Juliet and her enjoyment of the "love game," has also contributed to the tragedy. Tybalt, because of his temper and unwillingness to have Romeo remain at the Capulet ball, issued a challenge, which led to the

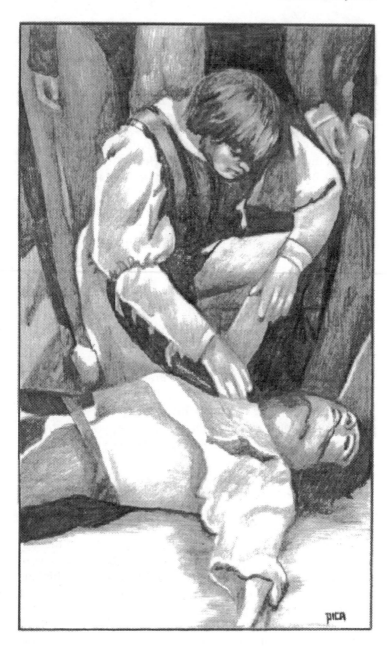

inevitability of a duel. Even Romeo's preoccupation with Juliet and his love contribute to reaching the climax of the play. These characters are all involved in the downfall of the lovers. However, none of them do so deliberately. Their basic character traits cause them to act and react in the manner that they do. While fate still has some role in these events, it is important to acknowledge that action proceeds inevitably from the nature of the characters and the conditions surrounding them.

Shakespeare has created three distinct personalities in the characters of Tybalt, Benvolio, and Mercutio. All the young men involved in the quarrel have contrasting temperaments. Tybalt is arrogant, proud, bad-tempered, and is called "Good King of Cats." Benvolio, on the other hand, is reasonable, offers good will to all, and is peace loving. It is interesting to note that he is the one who always tries to make peace, break up fights, and console his friends. It is Benvolio who relates to Lord Montague the details of the initial fight in the beginning of the play, and it is Benvolio who is asked by the Prince to relate the details of this deadly fight in Act III, Scene 1. Mercutio is portrayed as clever; smart; and a lover of words, puns, and figures of speech. He is able to joke even about death. When Mercutio is asked about his wound, he replies with a pun, a humorous use of a word to suggest two or more meanings, by stating, "No, 'tis not so deep as a well, nor so wide / as a church door; but 'tis enough, 'twill serve. Ask / for me tomorrow, and you shall find me a grave man." He is, in fact, so witty that no one takes him seriously when he is no longer joking.

Fate or chance again comes into play when the Prince gives Romeo his sentence. The law of Verona declares that if someone sheds blood, then his blood must be shed also. Because Tybalt killed Mercutio, he himself must be killed, and Romeo accomplished just that. However, Romeo has then shed blood. The Prince could have Romeo put to death, but he only banishes him.

The Nurse, in Scene 2, again misleads Juliet by not immediately telling her the news of Tybalt and Romeo. She weeps and cries out names and keeps Juliet guessing what has actually happened. The Nurse does not intentionally attempt to keep the news from Juliet, but she is overcome with grief. Her nature prevents her from telling Juliet the news in a calm and straightforward manner. When

Juliet first hears that Romeo is responsible for Tybalt's death, she feels deceived by his love. She answers the Nurse using oxymorons, "O serpent heart, hid with a flow'ring face!/ Did ever dragon keep so fair a cave?/ Beautiful tyrant! fiend angelical!/ Dove-feather'd raven! wolvish-ravening lamb!/ Despised substance of divinest show!/ Just opposite to what thou justly seem'st—/ A damned saint, an honourable villain!"

Juliet has divided emotions between her cousin and her husband, but when the nurse wishes grief, woes, and sorrows upon Romeo, Juliet rallies to Romeo's defense with the words, "Blister'd be thy tongue/ For such a wish! He was not born to shame. / Upon his brow shame is asham'd to sit;/ For 'tis a throne where honour may be crown'd/ Sole monarch of the universal earth." Juliet immediately realizes that her allegiance is with her husband. Even though she feels betrayed by him, she loves him deeply. Her love for him transcends even the grief of her cousin's death.

There is an ironic juxtaposition of love and death in these scenes. The values of love are represented by their marriage. This new love has caused Romeo to behave differently in the face of Tybalt's challenge and insults. And, set against this emotional love and well-being is the atmosphere of hate and revenge. After the death of Mercutio, Romeo realizes that his love has replaced his masculine characteristics. This leaves him feeling that he betrayed Mercutio by allowing him to fight what should have been his own fight. He states, "O sweet Juliet,/ Thy beauty hath made me effeminate/ And in my temper soft'ned valour's steel!" After the death of his friend, Romeo replaces his effeminate values of love with the masculine values of honor and revenge.

Shakespeare uses a number of allusions in this play, many of which are found in Scene 2 as Juliet waits for Romeo to come to her by night. Allusion is a reference to something in another work of literature, mythology, or history, and it is illustrated in the references to Phoebus Apollo, the Greek and Roman god of light.

Many examples of the theme of light and dark recur in these scenes. As Juliet is anxiously waiting for Romeo to come to her in scene 2, she gives a poetic praise of night when she states, "Come, night; come, Romeo; come, thou day in night;/ For thou wilt lie upon the wings of night/ Whiter than new snow upon a raven's back./ Come, gentle night; come, loving, black-brow'd night;/ Give me my Romeo; and, when he shall die,/ Take him and cut him out in little stars,/ And he will make the face of heaven so fine/ That all the world will be in love with night/ And pay no worship to the garish sun." The romantic night will give her her love who is illustrated as the brightness in the realm of blackness. Along with the images of dark and light is the reference to love and death co-existing side by side. Even in death, Juliet knows that he will continue to light the heavens in the form of stars.

Study Questions

1. Who begs Mercutio to leave the streets of Verona because the Capulets might also be out on this extremely hot day?

2. Who comes to the public square looking for a fight with Romeo?

3. What does Mercutio call Tybalt?

4. How does Tybalt insult Romeo and try to get him to fight him?

5. Why won't Romeo fight Tybalt?

6. Why does Mercutio fight Tybalt?

7. How is Mercutio killed?

8. Why does Romeo kill Tybalt?

9. Who tells the Prince about the murders?

10. What is Romeo's punishment?

Answers

1. Benvolio tries to get Mercutio to leave the streets of Verona because he is trying to prevent another fight.

2. Tybalt comes to the public square hoping to incite a fight with Romeo.

3. Mercutio calls Tybalt "Good King of Cats."

4. Tybalt insults Romeo by calling him a villain, hoping that this will cause him to fight.

5. Romeo will not fight Tybalt because now they are related by marriage. Tybalt is Juliet's cousin.

6. Mercutio fights Tybalt because he is angry that Tybalt is insulting Romeo, his friend.

7. Mercutio is killed when Romeo comes between them and blocks his view of Tybalt. Tybalt reaches under Romeo's arm and stabs Mercutio.

8. Romeo kills Tybalt because he feels that he must revenge his friend's death. After all, it was Romeo's fight and not Mercutio's.

9. Benvolio is the one who tells the Prince about the murders and relates exactly what happened.

10. Romeo's punishment is to be banished from Verona. If he is caught in the city of Verona, he will be put to death.

Suggested Essay Topics

1. Describe the events that foreshadow the death of Tybalt.

2. Define pun and explain how it is used in this act.

3. Act III is considered the climax of the plot. Explain why this is so.

4. Describe the character of Mercutio and the part he plays in the life of Romeo.

Act III, Scenes 3 and 4

Summary

Scene 3 takes place on Monday night inside Friar Laurence's cell. When Romeo fled the streets of Verona after the killings, he went there to hide. As the Friar approaches, the distraught Romeo asks what the Prince has decreed as his punishment.

The Friar says, "Not body's death, but body's banishment." To this, Romeo cries that banishment is worse than death because "There is no world without Verona walls." Friar Laurence attempts to make Romeo realize that he could have been sentenced to death, that the decree of banishment means that at least he will live. Romeo claims that not being able to see and touch Juliet is the same punishment as death. Romeo will not be consoled and throws himself on the floor in an extravagant display of grief.

The Nurse enters and is stern with Romeo. She says, "Stand up, stand up! Stand, and you be a man. / For Juliet's sake, for her sake, rise and stand! / Why should you fall into so deep an O?" At the sound of Juliet's name, Romeo inquires about her and asks if she hates him for killing her cousin. The nurse says that she is weeping and calling out both their names. Romeo grabs a knife, asks where in his anatomy does the name Montague lodge, and attempts to kill himself by cutting out that part.

The Nurse takes the dagger from Romeo, and the Friar accuses him of being womanish. The Friar gives Romeo three reasons why he should be glad that he is alive. One, Juliet is alive. Two, Tybalt could have killed him instead of the other way around. He should be happy that he (Romeo) is alive. Three, the Prince exiled Romeo instead of ordering his death. Friar Laurence then suggests a plan. Romeo is to visit Juliet that night as planned earlier. Then, he is to leave the city before daylight and travel to Mantua where he will stay until it is safe to return to Verona. The Friar will attempt to reconcile the feuding families, reveal the secret marriage, and obtain the Prince's pardon for Romeo which will allow him to return to Verona. The Nurse and Romeo are pleased with the plan. She gives Romeo Juliet's ring. The Friar warns Romeo once again that he must be out of the city before the break of day. Friar Laurence will keep in touch with Romeo through his servant and let him know how things are progressing in Verona.

Scene 4 takes place within the Capulet house where the reader finds Paris evidently asking for an answer to his suit of marriage to Juliet. Lord and Lady Capulet are present, and it is very late on Monday night. Lord Capulet tells Paris that under the circumstances of the day (the recent killings) they have not had the opportunity to discuss marriage with Juliet. Lord Capulet, thinking that Juliet will be obedient in his wishes, decides to go ahead and tell Paris that he will give his consent for them to marry on Thursday of that week. Lord Capulet asks Lady Capulet to tell Juliet the good news before she retires for bed.

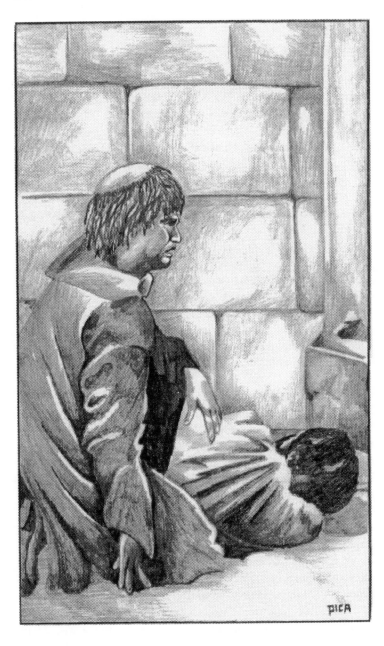

Analysis

Both Romeo and Juliet view his banishment as the worse kind of punishment. When Friar Laurence tells him the Prince's decree, Romeo states, "There is no world without Verona walls,/ But purgatory, torture, hell itself./ Hence-banished is banish'd from the world,/ And world's exile is death: then banished,/ Is death misterm'd; calling death banishment." Romeo realizes that his name has caused most of the complications in his life. Had his name not been Montague, he and Juliet could possibly have married with the blessings of both sets of parents. His anguish over killing Juliet's cousin causes him to become irrational. He draws his sword and states, "In what vile part of this anatomy/ Doth my name lodge? tell me that I may sack / The hateful mansion."

The Friar keeps Romeo from killing himself, but Romeo's attempted suicide is another example of his impulsiveness. He is very emotional and very rash in everything he does. His love with Juliet has been intense and fast and now appears to be destroyed. The love that he and Juliet share seems to be all consuming for both of them. It is not a courtly love and is not even considered a part of this world. Their love is so overwhelming that neither can imagine existing without the other. Death becomes the solution if they cannot be together.

The Nurse and Friar Laurence accept the news of death and banishment differently. True to her character, the Nurse is incoherent as she relates the news of Tybalt to Juliet; however, the Friar remains calm and philosophical concerning Romeo. These two characters begin to take on an even greater role in the lives of the lovers as they attempt to help and comfort them. It is the Friar who comes up with a plan to reunite the lovers for one last time. Friar Laurence only wants to help the lovers and ultimately end the feuding between the families. The Friar also realizes that he plays an important part in the consequences of the hastily arranged marriage performed by him. He must feel responsible for what has ultimately happened. His chances of reuniting the warring families looks rather bleak at this time.

The plot becomes intricate and complicated when Lord Capulet agrees to the marriage suit of Paris. He tells Paris, "I will make a desperate tender/ Of my child's love; I think she will be ruled/ In all respects by me; nay, more, I doubt it not." This announcement is not only significant for plot, but is an expression of patriarchal values, which are set against the freedom of love. Just as Romeo becomes a victim of societal values based on revenge and honor, so Juliet must submit to patriarchal authority in which women are always in subjection to their husbands or fathers. He has no idea that Juliet is already married, but assumes that she will be obedient to him and his requests. The customs of the day required her complete obedience. By arranging the marriage for Thursday, he unknowingly will force Juliet into more hasty actions. The plans of her father add new complications to Juliet's already troubled life.

Dramatic irony occurs when the audience knows that Juliet and Romeo are already married, and the characters on stage have no idea. Even as Lord Capulet gives his consent to Paris, they do not know that Romeo is with Juliet in her chamber.

Study Questions

1. What day is it in Scene 3?

2. Where did Romeo run to hide after the murder of Tybalt?

3. How does he react to the news that he is banished from Verona?

4. Who tells him that the Prince has banished him?

5. What upsets Romeo the most about being banished?

6. The Friar gives three reasons that Romeo should be happy. What were they?

7. What does the Nurse give to Romeo?

8. Where is Romeo to go before daybreak?

9. On what day does Lord Capulet plan for Juliet to be married to Paris?

10. Who is to tell Juliet the "good news" concerning her future marriage to Paris?

Answers

1. It is very late on Monday night in Scene 3.

2. After the murders, Romeo ran to hide in Friar Laurence's cell.

3. Romeo would rather die than be banished from Verona.

4. The Friar tells him the news that he will not be killed but only banished.

5. The thought of not seeing or touching Juliet ever again bothers Romeo the most.

6. The Friar gives Romeo three reasons for being happy: Juliet is alive; he is alive, and he is only banished not killed.

7. The Nurse gives Juliet's ring to Romeo.

8. Romeo must leave Juliet's bed chamber before daybreak and go to Mantua.

9. Lord Capulet has arranged for Juliet to marry Paris on Thursday.

10. Lady Capulet is to tell Juliet the "good news" before she retires to bed.

Suggested Essay Topics

1. Discuss Friar Laurence's plan to reunite Romeo and Juliet.

2. The nurse and Friar Laurence react differently to the situations presented in these scenes. Compare and contrast these reactions.

3. What events take place that complicate Juliet's life?

Act III, Scene 5

Summary

Scene 5 takes place very early Tuesday morning on day three. Romeo and Juliet have been together for the night and are discussing whether they hear the nightingale or the lark. The nightingale sings at night, and the lark sings in early morning. The child in Juliet insists that it is the nightingale, while Romeo insists that it is the lark, and he must hurry from the city. Juliet persuades him that it is the nightingale, and Romeo decides that he will stay longer, risking capture and even death. At this point, the more mature and fearful Juliet says that it is indeed the lark, and he must flee. They bid farewell, and Juliet has a vision that the next time that they see one another, he will be dead in a tomb.

Romeo leaves and Lady Capulet enters. Juliet is surprised by her mother's early visit and allows her mother to believe that her red eyes and wan appearance are the result of her weeping for Tybalt. Lady Capulet tells Juliet that she is going to send someone to Mantua to give Romeo poison. Then she tells her that she has good news for her. Her father has agreed to have her marry County Paris at Saint Peter's Church next Thursday.

Juliet says, "He shall not make me there a joyful bride!" Lord Capulet enters and notices the tears and asks if Lady Capulet has given her the news. Lady Capulet assures him that she told Juliet the news, and she (Juliet) wants nothing to do with Paris or the marriage.

Lord Capulet threatens Juliet and tells her that she will marry him or she can beg on the streets for all he cares, but she will inherit nothing from him. Juliet begs him for a delay, but he is angry and strong willed with her. He tells her that she will be at the church on Thursday even if he has to drag her there on a hurdle.

Juliet turns to her mother for help, and Lady Capulet says, "Do as thou wilt, for I have done with thee." When Lord and Lady Capulet leave, she turns to the nurse for help. The advice of the Nurse is to forget Romeo because he is banished. She recommends that Juliet marry Paris, who is "a lovely gentleman." To this advice, Juliet tells the Nurse that she is going to Friar Laurence's cell to make confession and be forgiven for her sins. Juliet is really going to seek his advice. If the Friar can not help her out of this situation, she has the power to kill herself rather than marry Paris.

Analysis

Within a matter of two days, Juliet has grown from an obedient child into a willful young woman. As morning comes after their wedding night together Juliet at first refuses to believe that it is the lark singing, because she cannot bear to have Romeo leave her.

Knowing that the lark sings at daybreak, and the nightingale sings at night, she wants to forestall daybreak when she knows that Romeo must leave. When Romeo says, "Let me be taken, let me be put to death," she becomes practical and aware of the danger. She then considers his safety before her desires and knows that it is time for him to leave. As Romeo leaves and she is looking down at him in the dawn of light, she says, "O God, I have an ill-divining soul!/ Methinks I see thee, now thou art below,/ As one dead in the bottom of a tomb;/ Either my eyesight fails, or thou look'st pale." Her premonition is a foreshadowing of the events to come.

The discussion between Lord and Lady Capulet and Juliet is extremely revealing. It allows the reader to see the coldness that exists between Juliet and her mother. There seems to be no closeness whatsoever. When Lady Capulet tells Juliet's father that she wants nothing to do with the marriage to Paris, Lord Capulet becomes angry. Juliet's mother tells him that "I would the fool were married to her grave!" Little did she know that she was foreshadowing the future for her daughter. Juliet pleads with her mother to help her delay the marriage, and her mother turns from her. Juliet attempts to persuade Lord Capulet to delay the marriage which causes him to become almost violent with her. He says, "Hang thee, young baggage! Disobedient wretch! / I tell thee what—get thee to church a Thursday / Or never after look me in the face. / Speak not, reply not, do not answer me! / My fingers itch." He goes on to rant and rave that she can beg, starve or die in the streets because he wants nothing to do with her if she does not consent to the marriage to Paris. He uses such insulting names as "greensickness," "carrion," "baggage," and "tallow-face" to describe his daughter. These are hardly words of endearment coming from her father. He cannot comprehend her disobeying him and is outraged at her sudden defiance.

Juliet delivers a brief soliloquy at the end of Act III as she expresses anger with the Nurse and announces that she will go consult with the Friar. Up until this point, the Nurse has been Juliet's confidant, counselor, and conspirator in her plans; however, her advice to marry Paris and forget Romeo has caused Juliet to seek help from someone else. By advising Juliet to forget Romeo and marry Paris, the Nurse totally loses Juliet's confidence. Juliet will

no longer confide in the Nurse or trust her. She has also enabled Juliet to become more independent and self-reliant.

By the end of Act III, both Romeo and Juliet have changed a great deal. Both lovers realize that the love that they have for one another is beyond this world of customs and parental involvement. Their love goes even beyond death, and they never waver in their fidelity. Rashness is still considered Romeo's tragic flaw. It is not his desire for revenge but the rashness of the revenge that was his undoing. Juliet's changes are demonstrated in her new determination and strength of character as she goes alone to Friar Laurence to seek advice.

Study Questions

1. On what day does Scene 5 take place?

2. What is significant about the lark and the nightingale?

3. What vision does Juliet have as Romeo is leaving?

4. Who comes to visit with Juliet early that morning?

5. What news does Lady Capulet give to Juliet?

6. What is Juliet's reaction to the news that Lady Capulet gives her?

7. Who does Juliet turn to for help when her parents leave?

8. What advice does the Nurse give Juliet?

9. Why does Juliet tell the Nurse that she is going to see Friar Laurence?

10. If the Friar cannot furnish a solution for Juliet, what does she have the power to do?

Answers

1. Scene 5 takes place on day three, a Tuesday morning.

2. The lovers are trying to determine the time of night or early morning. Romeo must be out of the city before daylight. The nightingale sings at night, while the lark sings in the early part of the morning.

3. Juliet has a vision that she sees Romeo as one dead in the bottom of a tomb.

4. Juliet's mother, Lady Capulet, comes to visit with her early that morning.

5. Lady Capulet brings Juliet the news that her father has consented for her to marry Paris on Thursday.

6. Juliet is upset and willfully says that she will not marry Paris. This is the first time she has been disobedient to her parents.

7. After her parents leave, Juliet turns to the Nurse for a solution to her dilemma.

8. The Nurse advises Juliet to forget Romeo, since he is banished, and marry Paris.

9. Juliet tells the Nurse that she is going to see Friar Laurence to confess her sins and get forgiveness. She is really going there to seek the Friar's help.

10. If Friar Laurence cannot help her, she has the power to commit suicide rather than marry Paris.

Suggested Essay Topics

1. Explain the relationship between Juliet and her parents. How has it changed from the beginning of the play?

2. Explain how Juliet has changed from the beginning of Act I up until Act III. Give examples of her behavior then and now.

3. Describe the role of the Nurse in Juliet's life. How does this role change in Act III?

4. What event forms the climax or turning point of the play, and what complications does this event create for Romeo and Juliet?

Act IV

Act IV, Scenes 1-3

Summary

As scene 1 opens, Paris is found at Friar Laurence's cell consulting with him about his wedding plans. The friar, who knows why this marriage can never take place, says that it is rushing to have the marriage on Thursday. Paris tells Friar Laurence that they have decided to go ahead and marry because Juliet has been weeping uncontrollably, and her father is worried about her. Lord Capulet, not knowing that she weeps for Romeo, believes that the marriage will help her get over Tybalt's death more quickly. Juliet arrives and Paris greets her as his wife. She responds coolly but cordially. After Paris tells her that he will come for her early Thursday morning, he departs. Juliet entreats the Friar to "come weep with me—past hope, past care, past help!"

The Friar tells her that he already knows the circumstances. Juliet explains that she would do anything to get out of the marriage to Paris and pleads for the friar to help her. She also tells him that if he cannot help, she will kill herself rather than marry Paris.

The Friar, realizing that she is serious about her feelings, tells her that he has a plan. She must go home, consent to marry Paris, and then she is to sleep alone on that Wednesday night before the wedding is to take place. When she is in bed, she is to drink a potion that he has made to induce sleep. The sleep will be so deep that no pulse can be found, and her body will be cold to the touch. The color will leave her face and she will appear as dead. She will stay in this condition 42 hours and then will awaken as from a pleasant sleep. When her family finds her early Thursday morning, they will take her to the family tomb where she will rest with Tybalt and those ancestors who have died. He, the Friar, will send letters to Romeo telling him of the plan, and he will be in the tomb waiting for her to awaken. Then, the two of them will go to Mantua.

Scene 2 finds Lord Capulet, the Nurse, and servants preparing for the wedding. Juliet returns from Friar Laurence's cell and goes directly to her father where she begs for his forgiveness. She says, "I beseech you! Henceforward I am ever ruled by you." Lord Capulet is so happy that she has returned to her original obedient nature that he sends for Paris to tell him that they can marry Wednesday instead of waiting for Thursday. Lord Capulet tells Lady Capulet to help Juliet, and he plans to stay up all night directing the servants in making preparations for the wedding that will take place in the morning, a day earlier than originally planned.

Scene 3 takes place within Juliet's chamber. She tells her mother that she needs no further help and that she needs to be left alone. As Juliet prepares to drink the potion, she becomes frightened and worries that if the potion does not work, she will have to marry Paris in the morning. To insure that this does not happen, she places her dagger beside her. A second worry is that possibly the potion is really poison, because the Friar might be afraid for his life since he was the one who married her to Romeo. A third worry is that she might awaken before Romeo gets there and because there is no air to breathe, she will suffocate. Her fourth worry is that she will awaken in the tomb, but the terror of the vault will be too much for her and she will lose her mind and kill herself.

Then she thinks she sees Tybalt's ghost coming for Romeo. It is this sight that enables her to summon up the courage to drink the potion.

Analysis

Act IV is considered the falling action of the play. The action moves swiftly and logically toward the tragedy that occurs at the end of the play. The consequences or forces that oppose the protagonists bring the ultimate end closer. The recent events have propelled the characters in one direction and the results are almost inevitable at this point. The tempo of the action increases

from this act until the end of the play.

Juliet is experiencing internal conflict throughout this act and especially in Scenes 1, 2, and 3. She has developed from a child into a woman who has fallen in love and married. She must act without Romeo and without the assistance of the nurse. She has disobeyed her parents by refusing to marry Paris, and lied about her reason for going to Friar Laurence's cell. She knows that she can not legally or morally marry Paris. Yet, she cannot tell her father about her marriage to Romeo. She also knows that by giving the impression of conformity and submitting to the wishes of her father, she can avoid any more confrontations and carry out the plan devised by the Friar. Her sense of betrayal by the nurse's advice to marry Paris has caused Juliet to feel that she has lost her closest friend and confidant. Juliet realizes that she must rely upon her own decisions and intuitions from now on. When she returns from Friar Laurence's cell and prepares to drink the potion, she is again struck with internal conflict. Her desperation is demonstrated by the fact that she places a dagger beside her in case the potion does not work. Rather than marry Paris, she will choose death.

Friar Laurence has become a pivotal character in the plot of the play. Some of his actions have been hasty and without proper reasoning. However, the Friar only wants good to come of his decisions. The reader was prepared for the use of the Friar's knowledge of herbs and plants from Act II, Scene 3. This knowledge will be used in the potion Juliet is to drink. He has become a confidant to not only Romeo, but also Juliet. He is patient with the lovers as they threaten suicide in place of being apart. He has kept them from suicide and helped to find a solution to the dilemma that surrounds them. He is a neutral character who tries to end the violence in his society; however, his plans will cause the deaths of a number of characters.

Scene 2 contrasts drastically with the preceding one which was centered upon desperation, talk of death, conflict, and trouble. In this scene, there are happy preparations for a celebration of marriage. It is a domestic scene full of excitement and promises of new beginnings. It is dramatic irony that the audience or reader knows that because of the sleeping potion Juliet will not be a part of the joy, preparations, or celebration.

Juliet's final speech before she drinks the potion is a good example of the Shakespearean soliloquy. She deliberates its pros and cons before drinking the liquid. She is afraid that the potion will not work. She fears that Friar Laurence has given her poison to cover his part in the secret marriage to Romeo. She is afraid of awakening in the burial vault before Romeo arrives and not being able to breathe, and finally, she is afraid of going mad amid the horrors of the skeletons and smells that will surround her.

Study Questions

1. Why is Paris at Friar Laurence's cell?

2. What reason does Paris give the Friar for the hasty marriage?

3. How long will the sleeping potion take effect?

4. Where will Juliet be put after her family believes that she is dead?

5. Who will be waiting in the tomb when Juliet awakens from the sleeping potion?

6. Who is supervising the preparations for the wedding?

7. What change does Lord Capulet make in the wedding plans?

8. If the potion does not work, what does Juliet plan to do?

9. What vision makes her have the strength to go ahead and drink the potion?

10. How will Romeo know about the plans?

Answers

1. Paris is arranging his wedding with Friar Laurence.

2. The marriage is hasty in order to stop Juliet's tears over Tybalt's death.

3. The sleeping potion will last for 42 hours.

4. After her parents think she is dead, Juliet will be placed in the Capulet vault with her deceased ancestors.

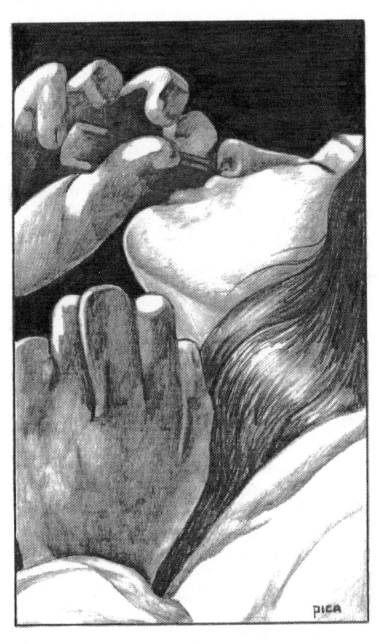

5. When Juliet awakens from the sleeping potion, Romeo will be waiting for her in the tomb.

6. Lord Capulet is supervising the wedding preparations.

7. Lord Capulet moves the wedding from Thursday to Wednesday.

8. If the potion does not work, she plans to kill herself with the dagger that she lays beside her.

9. The vision of Tybalt coming after Romeo gives her the strength to go ahead and drink the potion.

10. Romeo will know of the plan because Friar Laurence is planning to send him a letter.

Suggested Essay Topics

1. Write a character sketch of Juliet emphasizing the internal conflict she is experiencing in this act.

2. How has the Friar's hobby contributed to the plot of the play?

3. Discuss the four fears Juliet experiences just before she drinks the sleeping potion.

Act IV, Scenes 4 and 5

Summary

Scene 4 takes place in a hall of the Capulet's house. Lord and Lady Capulet, the Nurse, and numerous servants are busily preparing for the wedding. The Capulets and their servants are making jokes, not realizing that Juliet is in a deathlike trance in her room. She has risked her life in order to avoid what her family is celebrating. The curfew bell has just chimed three o'clock on Wednesday morning. Lord Capulet hears the music made by Paris and his company as they come for Juliet, and sends the Nurse to awaken and prepare her for the wedding.

Scene 5 is within Juliet's chamber. The Nurse comes into her room calling for her to get up because Paris is arriving. She calls

her a "slugabed," a sleepy head, and draws back the curtains surrounding her bed. She believes that Juliet is dead and begins
screaming. Lord and Lady Capulet rush into the room. Lord Capulet
looks at her and exclaims, "She's cold, / Her blood is settled, and
her joints are stiff; / Life and these lips have long been separated.
/ Death lies on her like an untimely frost." The Friar, Paris, and his
musicians enter, and Lord Capulet tells them that Juliet is dead,
and "Death is my son-in-law, Death is my heir; / My daughter he
hath wedded." The love that the Capulets have for their daughter
is indicated in the following lines: "Accursed, unhappy, wretched,
hateful day!/ Most miserable hour that e'er time saw/ In lasting
labour of his pilgrimage!/ But one, poor one, one poor and loving
child,/ But one thing to rejoice and solace in,/ And cruel death hath
catch'd it from my sight!" The anguish seems to be genuine even
though earlier in the play Juliet's parents had wished that she "were
married to her grave." The lines that Lord and Lady Capulet say
are repetitive and exaggerated. Their grief does not raise sympa-
thy in the audience or reader because of the knowledge that Juliet
is not really dead.

The Friar, knowing that she is not really dead, attempts to comfort them by saying that they have done their part. Now, she be-
longs solely to Heaven. He consoles them and tells them to dry their
eyes for she is better off in heaven. Lord Capulet decrees that everything that was to celebrate a wedding is to be changed befitting
a funeral. The happiness of the wedding music will be changed to
"melancholy bells." The hymns will change to dirges, and the bridal
flowers will now become funeral flowers.

The scene ends with a comic discussion between the musicians and Peter.

Analysis

Compared to the volatile scene when Juliet refuses to marry
Paris, Lord and Lady Capulet behave quite differently when they
believe that she is dead. Lady Capulet's last words in Act III were "I
would the fool were married to her grave!" Little did she realize
that she was foreshadowing the future for her daughter. Lord
Capulet, also, changed during the course of the play. In Act I, Lord
Capulet tells Paris that "She is the hopeful lady of my earth." All his

other children are dead and his life revolves around her; yet, he refuses to consider her feelings. Act III illustrates the anger and vengeance he threatens to take out on her if she does not marry Paris, and then, in Act IV, he swings full circle back to the doting and loving father. The Capulets' flaws center on their egos. They become too assured that they alone know what is best for their daughter. They do not have a close relationship with her and communicate poorly. In spite of these character flaws, they do love their only remaining child, and want what they believe to be the best for her.

It is interesting to watch the Friar lovingly and patiently console the parents because he knows all the circumstances. Some critics have wondered if the friar might be afraid of admitting his part in the uniting of the lovers because of the feud between the families.

There are many instances of dramatic irony in this act. Dramatic irony is a contrast between the audience's understanding of words and actions and the character's understanding. Juliet's meeting with Paris in Friar Laurence's cell is one example. Juliet is there to seek help in avoiding the very marriage that Paris is there trying to arrange. Another example are the wedding preparations by Lord Capulet. The Capulets and their servants are making jokes and busily preparing for the wedding, and the bride lies in her room in a deathlike trance. He is preparing for gaiety and happiness, and Juliet has taken a deathlike sleeping potion. The wedding arrangements will change into funeral arrangements. The ironic imagery of Juliet as the bride of death is illustrated in the lines, "The night before thy wedding-day/ Hath Death lain with thy wife. There she lies,/ Flower as she was, deflowered by him./ Death is my son-in-law, Death is my heir;/ My daughter he hath wedded." The emphasis on this tragic reversal anticipates the ending and is an example of tragedy as a reversal of expectations.

The final scene with Peter and the musicians provides the audience with comic relief. These men are not involved in Juliet's death and illustrate the fact that ordinary life goes on in spite of tragedy. Peter, who is himself a servant, enjoys making the musicians subservient to him.

Study Questions

1. Scene 4 takes place at what time in the morning?

2. Scene 4 takes place on what day?

3. How do the Capulets know that Paris is approaching?

4. Who is sent to wake up Juliet?

5. What does the Nurse find?

6. Who tries to console the Capulets by saying that Juliet is better off in heaven?

7. How do the wedding preparations change after they find Juliet?

8. How does the County Paris react to the death of Juliet?

9. How does Lord Capulet know that she is dead?

10. How does the act end?

Answers

1. Scene 4 takes place at three in the morning.

2. Scene 4 takes place early on Wednesday morning.

3. The Capulets know that Paris is coming because they can hear the music of his musicians.

4. The Nurse is sent to wake up Juliet.

5. The Nurse finds Juliet "dead" in her bed chamber.

6. The Friar tries to console the Capulets by assuring them that Juliet is in heaven.

7. The wedding preparations change dramatically. The wedding music becomes funeral dirges. The wedding flowers become funeral flowers, and the happiness associated with a wedding becomes sadness.

8. Paris is devastated by the news that Juliet is dead. He says, "Beguiled, divorced, wronged, spited, slain! / Most detest-

able Death, by thee beguiled, / By cruel, cruel thee quite over-thrown. / O love! O life! not life, but love in death!"

9. Lord Capulet believes that Juliet is dead because he feels that her body is cold to the touch and her joints are stiff.

10. Act IV ends with a comic discussion between the musicians and Peter.

Suggested Essay Topics

1. Describe the reactions of Lord Capulet, Lady Capulet, the Nurse, and Friar Laurence to the death of Juliet.

2. Define dramatic irony and give examples from this act.

Act V

Act V, Scenes 1 and 2

New Characters:

Balthasar: *a servant to Romeo*

Apothecary: *a druggist in Mantua who is extremely poor*

Friar John: *a Franciscan friar who is a friend to Friar Laurence*

Summary

Romeo is waiting for Balthasar to arrive with news from Verona. He is in Mantua and it is Thursday. He has had a dream that Juliet finds him dead, and she brings him back to life as an emperor with her kisses. Balthasar arrives telling Romeo that he saw Juliet buried in the Capulet tomb. Romeo says, "Then I defy you, stars!" and makes a hasty plan. He orders Balthasar to hire some fast horses and bring him ink and paper. Romeo inquires if there is a letter from the friar, and when the servant answers negatively, Romeo orders him to get what he demanded.

Romeo remembers an Apothecary in Mantua who appears to be extremely poor. Romeo decides to go to him and try to buy poison. It is against the law to sell poison in Mantua, but Romeo thinks he can sway the Apothecary to sell it to him because of his (the Apothecary's) extreme poverty.

Romeo offers the apothecary 40 ducats or gold pieces for the poison. At first, the man refuses to sell him the liquid, but reconsiders after Romeo reminds him of his extreme poverty. The Apothecary tells Romeo how to administer the poison, and Romeo replies, "There is thy gold—worse poison to men's souls. / Doing more murder in this loathsome world, / Than these poor compounds that thou mayst not sell. / I sell thee poison; thou hast sold me none." After buying the poison, Romeo plans to go to Juliet's grave and die with her.

Scene 2 takes place in Friar Laurence's cell where he is welcoming Friar John from Mantua. Friar Laurence asks if there is a letter from Romeo, and Friar John tells him that he was not able to go to Mantua after all. While he was visiting the sick, the city authorities were afraid that the sickness might be the plague and quarantined the house. He was not allowed to leave the house or give the letter to a messenger to return to the Friar. Friar Laurence realizes that Romeo knows nothing of the plan to meet Juliet in the tomb and fears the worst. He asks Friar John to bring him a crow bar quickly, and he prepares to leave for the Capulet tomb where Juliet will be waking up within the next three hours.

Analysis

Events involving chance, circumstance, and coincidence in tragedy reinforce the notion of fate, and are considered beyond human control and contrary to men's best intentions. It is a coincidence that there happens to be a poor Apothecary who consents to sell Romeo the poison even if it is against the law. It is a matter of chance that the important letter relating the plans for Romeo and Juliet was not delivered by Friar John. The need for the delivery is coincident with the delay caused by the quarantine. Coincidence is also involved when Balthasar reports Juliet's death to Romeo before a true report is received from the friar. Romeo has no way of knowing that she is not dead. From this false knowledge, Romeo, being impetuous, acts too hastily and rushes to the Apothecary to purchase poison in order that he might die with Juliet. Through fate or the use of chance, circumstance, or coincidence, the resolution or conclusion of Act V is now inevitable.

Dreams and premonitions in the play, like foreshadowing, intensify the work of fate. Romeo has a dream of death in which he says,"My dreams presage some joyful news at hand;/ My bosom's lord sits lightly in his throne;/ And all this day an unaccustom'd spirit/ Lifts me above the ground with cheerful thoughts./ I dreamt

my lady came and found me dead/ Strange dream, that gives a dead man leave to think/ And breathed such life with kisses in my lips,/ That I revived, and was an emperor." His dream of death is soon to be fulfilled and Juliet will kiss him on the lips. She will not awaken him, but she will join him in death.

The sickness that was so feared by the authorities that it caused them to quarantine Friar John was the bubonic plague. This plague killed millions of people in Europe, and its causes were not understood by the people. It is ironic that the authorities, through a fear of death by the plague, kept Friar John from delivering the letter, because the undelivered letter caused many deaths not related to the plague.

Romeo always considered suicide the final solution if he cannot live with Juliet. Thus, it is no surprise that, upon learning of Juliet's "death," he immediately goes to purchase poison. After Romeo buys the poison he says, "Come, cordial and not poison, go with me/ To Juliet's grave; for there must I use thee." Romeo's verbal irony is that the poison, because it will reunite him with Juliet, is really a restorative medicine. It was believed that a "cordial" was a kind of medicine that restored the heartbeat.

Study Questions

1. Where does Scene 1 take place?

2. What was Romeo's dream?

3. Who brings Romeo the news that Juliet is dead?

4. Why does Romeo go to the Apothecary?

5. How much does Romeo pay for the poison?

6. Why does the Apothecary hesitate in selling Romeo the poison?

7. What persuades the Apothecary to go ahead and sell Romeo the poison?

8. Who does Friar Laurence entrust with the important letter to Romeo?

9. Why is the letter not delivered to Romeo?

10. How long will it be before Juliet wakes up?

Answers

1. Scene 1 takes place in Mantua where Romeo has been banished.

2. Romeo dreams that Juliet finds him dead and brings him back to life as an emperor with her kisses.

3. Balthasar, Romeo's servant, brings him the news that Juliet is dead and was buried in the Capulet tomb.

4. Romeo goes to the Apothecary to buy poison.

5. Romeo pays 40 ducats for the poison.

6. The Apothecary hesitates in selling Romeo the poison because it is against the law in Mantua to sell the substance.

7. Because of his extreme poverty, the Apothecary consents to sell Romeo the poison.

8. Friar Laurence entrusts the important letter to Friar John to deliver to Romeo. This letter explains to Romeo about Juliet's pretended death and tells him to be at the tomb when she wakes up.

9. Friar John is not able to deliver the letter because he is quarantined while visiting the sick.

10. Juliet is due to wake up in about three hours.

Suggested Essay Topics

1. What coincidences occur in this act?

2. Explain fully what goes wrong with Friar Laurence's plan to reunite the lovers.

Act V, Scene 3

New Characters:

Page: *a servant to Paris*

Summary

Scene 3 takes place in the churchyard where the Capulet monument is located. Paris and the Page are outside the tomb of Juliet. Paris instructs the page to put out the torch and stand guard while he enters the tomb. The Page is to whistle if anyone approaches. As Paris begins to enter the tomb the Page whistles, indicating that someone is near. Paris watches as Romeo and Balthasar approach. Romeo instructs Balthasar to give a letter to his father the next morning and not to intervene with his purpose. Romeo tells Balthasar that the reason he is at the tomb is to look upon Juliet's face and to remove a ring from her finger. Balthasar is then instructed to leave the churchyard under the penalty of death by Romeo if he fails to obey him.

Balthasar does not believe Romeo's reasons for being at the tomb and fears for his master. Because of his concern for Romeo, Balthasar hides nearby rather than leave the churchyard.

As Romeo enters the tomb, Paris recognizes him as Romeo, the one who killed Tybalt and caused Juliet so much grief. Paris believes that he has come to the tomb to do some "vile outrage" to the bodies of Tybalt and Juliet. He steps forward and tries to prevent Romeo from entering the tomb. Because Paris has no torch, Romeo does not recognize him. They fight, and Paris is killed. As they fight, the Page runs for help. After Paris falls fatally wounded, Romeo looks upon his face and realizes that it is Paris. He remembers Balthasar telling him something about Juliet being promised to marry Paris, so he decides to bury him also in the tomb with Juliet. Romeo drags Paris' body into the Capulet tomb and goes to Juliet's side.

As he embraces Juliet, Romeo talks about her beauty even in death. Her lips and cheeks are crimson, and he notices that even Death cannot take away her beauty. He embraces her, kisses her one last time, and joins her in death by drinking the poison.

At this point, Friar Laurence enters the churchyard and stumbles upon Balthasar who is hiding. Balthasar tells the friar that Romeo has been in the tomb about half an hour and he is afraid. The Friar is afraid that something has happened and rushes into the tomb. He finds the bodies of Paris and Romeo. Juliet is just beginning to stir, and upon recognizing the friar, she asks about Romeo. The Friar hears the night guard coming and knowing that he could be implicated in the murder, becomes frightened and begs Juliet to accompany him outside. He tells her that their plans have gone awry and Paris, as well as Romeo, are dead. He promises to take her to a place where nuns live. Juliet refuses to leave and the friar, rather than be discovered, does not even stay to help Juliet, but flees.

Juliet notices the cup in Romeo's hand and knows that it is poison that has ended her lover's life. She tries to drink just one drop to kill herself, but she finds nothing left in the cup. She kisses him and realizes that his lips are still warm. Upon hearing the watchmen approaching, she takes Romeo's dagger and kills herself.

The watchmen enter the tomb and find the bodies of Paris, Romeo, and Juliet, who supposedly died two days ago. Yet, her body is warm and newly dead. The Capulets and the Montagues are sent for as the watchmen begin to bring in suspects. One watchman brings Balthasar into the tomb, and another watchman finds Friar Laurence. The Prince arrives and inquires about the deaths. When the Capulets arrive, Lord Capulet notices that Romeo's dagger is the one that was used to kill his daughter and assumes that Romeo is responsible for her death. Lord Montague enters and tells the Prince that grief over Romeo's exile has also caused Lady Montague's death.

The Prince demands that the cries of vengeance be stopped until the truth can be discovered. He orders that the "parties of suspicion" be brought forward. The Friar admits to being the most suspected because he was caught leaving the churchyard carrying instruments to break into a tomb. Finally the Friar is forced to relate the entire story concerning Romeo and Juliet. He tells how they were married and her father demanded that she marry Paris. He

tells of the plan for Juliet to drink the sleeping potion, be reunited with Romeo after 42 hours, and the accidental quarantine that prevented his letter from reaching Romeo. The Friar accepts the responsibility for what has happened and says, "Let my old life be sacrificed some hour before his time / Unto the rigor of severest law." The Prince says that Friar Laurence is a holy man and turns to question Balthasar.

Balthasar tells the Prince how he brought news of Juliet's death to Romeo in Mantua. He relates how they arrived at the tomb and Romeo gave him the letter that was to have gone to Lord Montague the next morning.

The Page is then instructed to tell his side of the story. He relates how his master came to Juliet's grave to bring flowers and weep. Paris was startled when Romeo approached the tomb, and fearing that Romeo wanted to do some damage to the bodies, tried to arrest him. Paris and Romeo fought and Paris was killed.

After reading the letter, the Prince declares that all the Friar had said was true. Because of the hatred between the Capulets and Montagues, both sides have lost many loved ones. The Capulets and Montagues shake hands and decide to build gold statues in honor of their children. Their children were "poor sacrifices of our enmity." The play ends with the Prince saying that there was never a story sadder than the one of Romeo and Juliet.

Analysis

The conclusion or catastrophe takes place in Scene 3 of the play. The conclusion quickly draws to a close as almost all the characters are on stage for various reasons. This last scene reveals one death not witnessed and three that are performed on stage. The predictions issued at the beginning of the play by the Chorus have all been fulfilled. Each scene contributes to the plot and focuses on the lovers' plight. This scene contains more examples of fate or coincidence and how it controlled the lives of the lovers.

Some illustrations of the workings of fate through chance or coincidence are Romeo's suicide just before Juliet awakens, Friar Laurence arriving just a little too late to save him, and even Juliet's death. If Romeo had not been so hasty, he would have realized that Juliet was not dead. Just a small hesitation on his part would have

allowed her to awaken. Again, Romeo and Juliet's hastiness play a part in their destruction. The deaths are not only a testimony to the force of fate working through chance, coincidence, change or reversal, circumstance, and personal flaws, but to the power of their love.

Again, light transforms the darkness when he first sees Juliet in the tomb and says, "For here lies Juliet, and her beauty makes/ This vault a feasting presence full of light." The love that they saw in one another's presence was a source of warmth and light. The theme of light and dark is present even in the last scene of the play.

Irony also plays a part as the families honor the lovers in death although they would have refused to recognize their love while they were alive. Romeo and Juliet lived in a culture that was unsympathetic toward love and idealism. The violence and hatred present in their society naturally bred tragedy.

Romeo's speech as he opens the Capulet tomb contains many examples of metaphorical language. He says, "Thou detestable maw, thou womb of death, / Gorged with the dearest morsel of the earth, / Thus I enforce thy rotten jaws to open, / And in despite I'll cram thee with more food." Romeo is comparing the tomb to a detestable maw, and a womb of death. The dearest morsel of the earth is referring to Juliet and the jaws refer to the mouth of the tomb itself. His death fulfills the reference of cramming the tomb with more food. Death is personified as her love—an image foreshadowed earlier.

In the final scene, the Prince says, "See what a scourge is laid upon your hate, / That heaven finds means to kill your joys with love." It is ironic that love could kill joy, but the love shared by Romeo and Juliet ultimately ended their lives. Romeo and Juliet were the "joys" of the Montague and Capulet families. It was because of the hate between the families that the children were afraid to make their love known.

One of the causes of this tragedy is that the flaw of impulsiveness is shared by many of the characters. Friar Laurence, Tybalt, Lord Capulet, Romeo, Mercutio, Juliet, and even the Nurse all contribute to the tragedy through impulsiveness, which is the real villain in the play. Shakespeare illustrated the rashness in the old and young alike in a universal way. Chance or fate plays a role in this tragedy, but the importance of character and the actions stemming from it are equally important. The connection of character with his deed and then to the tragedy sets the course for the catastrophe, and its outcome is inevitable.

The universality of Shakespeare's plays make the reader or audience realize that time does not alter human nature, and Romeo and Juliet have become symbols of youthful romance. Hate breeds violence and death, and love can transcend all earthly rules and boundaries.

Study Questions

1. Why is Paris at Juliet's tomb?
2. What is Paris' last request?
3. Why does Paris think Romeo has come to the Capulet tomb?
4. Who kills Paris?
5. If Romeo had not been so hasty in drinking the poison, what would he have noticed about Juliet?
6. Name the people who have died in this scene.
7. Where does Friar Laurence want to take Juliet?
8. How does Juliet kill herself?
9. Who is suspected the most as a murderer and why?
10. What four accounts does the Prince hear?

Answers

1. Paris has come to Juliet's tomb to bring flowers and weep.
2. As he dies, Paris' last request is to lie beside Juliet.
3. Paris believes that Romeo has come to the tomb to do damage to the bodies of Tybalt and Juliet.
4. Romeo kills Paris.
5. If Romeo had not been so hasty in drinking the poison, he would have understood why Juliet's lips and cheeks were crimson. She was beginning to wake up from the potion.

6. Paris, Lady Montague, Romeo, and Juliet have all died in this scene.

7. When Juliet wakes up, Friar Laurence is there and wants to take her to a "sisterhood of holy nuns."

8. Juliet kills herself with Romeo's dagger.

9. Friar Laurence is suspected the most because he is carrying tools for digging and opening tombs.

10. When the Prince wants to know what has happened, Friar Laurence, Balthasar, the Page, and the contents of the letter in Balthasar's possession all give the same account of the events.

Suggested Essay Topics

1. Describe the role of Friar Laurence in the play and how he contributes to the fate of the lovers.

2. Explain in detail how Romeo and Juliet both mature during the course of the play. Cite examples from their speech or actions that illustrate your position.

3. How have the deaths of Romeo and Juliet affected the entire city of Verona?

4. Discuss the role of chance or coincidence in the play. How did it affect the ending of the play?

5. Discuss the role of Paris in the play.

Sample Analytical Paper Topics

The following paper topics are based on the entire play. Following each topic is a thesis and sample outline. Use these as a starting point for your paper.

Topic #1

Impetuosity is a tragic flaw that affects character and action. This flaw within a character will ultimately cause the death of the protagonist. Write an essay in which hasty decisions or actions result in the final tragedy of the play.

Outline

I. Thesis Statement: *Impetuosity is a tragic flaw present in the characters of Romeo, Juliet, Lord Capulet, and Friar Laurence.*

II. Impetuosity of Romeo

    A. Love

        1. Instant love for Juliet

        2. Decision to marry

        3. Preference to death rather than be parted from Juliet

    B. Relationship with others

        1. Reaction after he is banished

        2. Kills Tybalt

        3. Kills Paris

        4. Purchase of poison from the apothecary

III. Impetuosity of Juliet

   A. Love

      1. Instant love for Romeo

      2. Decision to marry

      3. Her death

   B. Relationship to others

      1. Reactions after learning that she is to marry Paris

      2. Her attitude toward her parents

IV. Impetuosity of Lord Capulet

   A. Decision to give consent for Juliet to marry Paris

   B. Reaction when Juliet refuses to marry Paris

   C. Decision to move the date up one day

V. Impetuosity of Friar Laurence

   A. Willingness to marry Romeo and Juliet

   B. Sending Friar John with the letter to Romeo instead of Balthasar

   C. Leaving Juliet in the tomb after she awoke

VI. Conclusion: Romeo, Juliet, Lord Capulet, and Friar Laurence all acted hastily at some point in the play which contributed to the final destruction of Romeo and Juliet.

Topic #2

Because the entire play represents only five days in the lives of Romeo and Juliet, the time line is an important element. Write an essay explaining the happenings on each of these days and explain how these influenced the outcome of the play.

Outline

I. Thesis Statement: *Important situations occur in each of these five days of the protagonists' lives that influence the outcome of the play.*

II.   Day One—Sunday

   A.   The quarrel among the Capulet and Montague servants

        1.   Tybalt fights Benvolio

        2.   Prince issues warning

   B.   Romeo's romantic nature

        1.   His infatuation for Rosaline

        2.   His love for Juliet is established

   C.   Paris asks to marry Juliet

   D.   Lord Capulet's ball

        1.   Romeo and Juliet meet

        2.   Tybalt's anger is ignited against Romeo

III. Day Two—Monday

   A.   Romeo incorporates Friar Laurence's help

   B.   The Nurse meets with Romeo to get the wedding plans

   C.   Romeo and Juliet are married

   D.   The fights on the streets of Verona

        1.   Tybalt kills Mercutio

        2.   Romeo kills Tybalt

   E.   Romeo is banished

   F.   Friar Laurence devises a plan for Romeo and Juliet

   G.   Paris is granted permission to marry Juliet

IV.   Day Three—Tuesday

   A.   Juliet refuses to marry Paris

   B.   Friar Laurence devises another plan for Juliet

        1.   Juliet drinks the sleeping potion

        2.   Friar Laurence sends a message to Romeo

V.   Day Four—Wednesday

   A.   Juliet is found "dead"

    B.   Juliet is buried in the Capulet monument

VI. Day Five—Thursday

    A.   Romeo learns of Juliet's death

    B.   Romeo buys poison

    C.   Romeo kills Paris and himself

    D.   Friar Laurence learns that his message to Romeo was not delivered

    E.   Juliet kills herself

VII. Conclusion: The plot of Romeo and Juliet is developed in the course of five days in the lives of the protagonists.

Topic #3

The structure of a play is important to the development and ultimate resolution of the conflict. Write an essay in which the five stages of a tragedy are examined showing a relationship to the story and its development.

Outline

I.   Thesis Statement: *A tragedy can be organized by the dramatist into five components of dramatic structure which enable the play to progress smoothly and logically to a conclusion.*

II.   Introduction or exposition

    A.   Tone is established.

        1.   Feud between the families

        2.   Love of Romeo and Rosaline

        3.   Love of Romeo and Juliet

    B.   Setting is evoked.

        1.   Streets of Verona

        2.   Capulet household

    C.   Characters are introduced.

III. Complication or rising action

    A.   Love between the children of the two feuding families

    B.   Marriage of Romeo and Juliet

    C.   Tybalt's challenge to Romeo

IV. Climax or Turning Point

    A.   The murders

        1.   Mercutio

        2.   Tybalt

    B.   Romeo's banishment

    C.   Lord Capulet's decree that Juliet is to marry Paris

V.   Falling Action

    A.   Juliet's internal conflict

        1.   Conflict with her parents

        2.   Conflict with the nurse

        3.   Conflict concerning the compulsory marriage to Paris

        4.   Fears concerning the potion

    B.   Friar Laurence's plan for Romeo and Juliet

VI. Conclusion or catastrophe

    A.   Friar Laurence's message does not reach Romeo

    B.   Deaths

        1.   Paris

        2.   Romeo

        3.   Juliet

    C.   Feud ends with the deaths of Romeo and Juliet

VII. Conclusion: The introduction, the complication, the climax, the falling action, and the conclusion are components of dramatic structure which enable the play to progress smoothly and logically to a conclusion.

Topic #4

Fate and coincidence are used extensively in *Romeo and Juliet.* Both these elements helped to bring about the tragedy or destruction of the protagonists. Write an essay in which you give examples of how each element is used.

Outline

I. Thesis Statement: *The elements of fate—chance, circumstance, and coincidence—are used in* Romeo and Juliet *to advance the plot and bring about the ultimate deaths of the protagonists.*

II. Examples of chance and circumstance

    A. Romeo and Juliet are children of parents who hate one another

    B. The servant given the list of names for Lord Capulet's ball cannot read

    C. Benvolio is able to talk Romeo into attending the ball to look at Rosaline

    D. Lord Capulet allows Romeo to remain at the ball

    E. Romeo meets and falls in love with Juliet

    F. The lovers are separated because of an accidental fight

    G. The Prince decrees that Romeo is to be banished instead of put to death

III. Examples of coincidence

    A. Romeo is asked to read the invitation list for the illiterate servant

    B. Tybalt recognizes Romeo's voice at the ball

    C. Lord Capulet moves the wedding day from Thursday to Wednesday

    D. Balthasar happens to see Juliet's funeral and tells Romeo of her death

    E. Friar John is quarantined and Friar Laurence's message never reaches Romeo

    F.   Friar Laurence arrives too late at Juliet's tomb.

IV.   Conclusion: The elements of fate work hand in hand with each other to bring about the inevitable deaths of the protagonists.

Topic #5

    Comic relief is used by Shakespeare to delight his audiences. It is often used after an intense scene to relieve the tension brought about by the extremely emotional dialogue or actions in the play. Write an essay describing the situations when comic relief or humor was used by different characters in Shakespeare's *Romeo and Juliet*.

Outline

I.   Thesis Sentence: *The use of comic relief or humor is used predominately by three of Shakespeare's characters to relieve some of the moments of tension in* Romeo and Juliet.

II.   Nurse

    A.   Her compulsion to talk

    B.   Her use of malapropisms

    C.   Her teasing of Juliet

III.   Mercutio

    A.   His Queen Mab speech

    B.   The exchange between Benvolio and Mercutio in Act II, Scene 1

    C.   His use of puns and figurative language

IV.   Lord Capulet

    A.   His remarks toward the young ladies at his ball

    B.   His behavior at the ball

    C.   His preparations for the wedding

V.   Conclusion: Humor is used as a comic relief by the nurse, Mercutio, and Lord Capulet in order to relieve the tension brought about by more intense scenes or situations.

SECTION EIGHT

Bibliography

Craig, Hardin, Ed. *The Complete Works of Shakespeare.* Chicago: Scott, Foresman and Company, 1961.

Kittredge, George Lyman, Ed. *The Kittredge-Players Edition of the Complete Works of William Shakespeare.* New York: Grolier, 1936.

Prentice Hall Literature: Gold. New Jersey: Prentice Hall, Inc., 1989.

Toor, David. *A Life of Shakespeare.* New York: Kenilworth Press, 1976.

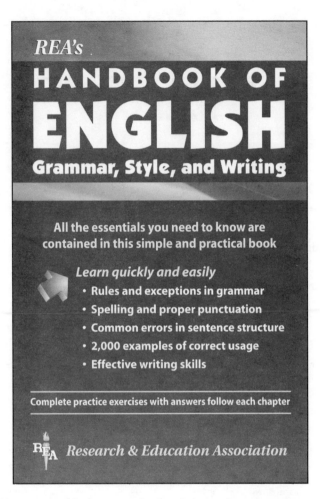